Leading Children in Worship

Leading Children in Worship

Bible Stories and Lesson Plans
Book 2

Helene G. Zwyghuizen

Baker Books

A Division of Baker Book House Co
Grand Rapids, Michigan 49516

Published by Baker Books
a division of Baker Book House Company
P.O. Box 6287, Grand Rapids, MI 49516-6287

Printed in the United States of America

ISBN 0-8010-5269-6

This book is dedicated to our children and grandchildren:

Keith and Ardith Doorenbos
Stephen Edward Doorenbos
Michael and Jayne French
Amanda Kaye French
Heidi Zwyghuizen
Edward and Melanie Zwyghuizen
Gabriel Andrew Zwyghuizen

Thank you for your love, encouragement, and support. Two parents could not have received greater children, in-laws, and grandchildren than those God has given us. We love you all!

Contents

Lent Series for Year Five

Lent Series for Year Six

Part Three: Two Prayer Series

Prayer Series for Younger Children

Prayer Series for Older Children

Part Four: Stories from the Book of Acts

Part Five: Patterns and Instructions

Part Six: Leader Resources

Acknowledgments

It is only right to give credit to Sofia Cavaletti for introducing us to the children-in-worship concept in her book, *The Religious Potential of the Child.* I reread it often to refresh my spirit and reset my sights. Dr. Jerome Berryman has expanded the basic idea in his books *Young Children and Worship,* which he wrote in collaboration with Dr. Sonja Stewart, and *Godly Play,* which I also reread.

Thank you to the members of Abbe Reformed Church, who pray for and encourage the children-in-worship ministry; who make shelves, desert boxes, figures, underlays, backgrounds, and enriching activities; who give baskets, trays, cards, shoe boxes, and the other needed supplies we ask for from time to time; and who help in so many ways.

A special thanks to our faithful and dedicated leaders and helpers who lead the children all year round. Your faithful preparation and tireless giving of your time and energy is inspiring. At Abbe Church, Sunday school meets every Sunday, year round, so your dedication is especially significant.

This book would not be possible without a special group of children who have worshiped with me for five years. All of the stories in this book with the exception of the two summer series, the Noah Stories and the Prayer Series for Younger Children, were written for these children: Sandy Persons, Christopher Legters, Travis White, Bryan Nickerson, Jenna White, and Nicole Schurman. Other children have joined us and others have moved up to other classes, but this group has been my core group since the fall of 1990. Thank you, children, for helping Mrs. Z. learn so much.

I would like to thank the following for giving us permission to use their material in this book:

Reverend Van Rathbun, who wrote "Manna and Water"; Donna Kling, who wrote "Moses' Helpers"; and Sybil Towner, whose "Guidelines for Leaders and Helpers" I adapted.

A special thank you to my husband, John E. Zwyghuizen, for designing and drawing up the plans for the ark, table, bed, temple, and stable and for giving me so much support, understanding, and love.

Thank you to our son Edward for drawing the layouts for each of the stories included in this book.

My deepest appreciation is due Betty DeVries, Mary Suggs, and all others at Baker Book House for shepherding with great skill this book through its various stages to completion.

To God, our Heavenly Father, belongs the praise, honor, and glory. My prayer is that the many who use these stories will come to know him as their own Savior and then go out and bring others to a saving faith so that the Kingdom of God continues to grow!

Introduction

Children in Worship

The children-in-worship approach helps children and adults experience the presence of God in the context of religious language. It provides an environment filled with the presence and power of God's love where the children and leader encounter God together. Because all of the senses are used, children learn their Bible stories very well. They learn the facts of each story and also the deeper truths of God's Word as leader and children or parent and child together worship God.

The Bible stories in this book can be used whenever children are gathered—during junior church time, as a Sunday school curriculum, on Wednesday evenings, for vacation Bible school, and during religion release times. Parents who are home schooling, want to make Bible stories come alive for their children, or have summer backyard Bible clubs will find these stories just what they need. Teachers in Christian preschools and elementary schools are using these stories in their classrooms. Missionaries in various countries have found these stories an effective method for leading people to Christ and discipling new Christians.

Wherever these Bible stories are used, children and adults learn to quietly enter the Worship Center and sit in the opening circle where they begin their approach to God. This time includes the greeting, the call to worship, and songs of praise.

The leader and children sit on the floor, folding their hands or holding their knees. We say "hug your hands" or "hug your knees" because of the loving feeling that gives. Masking tape on the floor or carpet samples arranged in a circle give the outline for sitting on the floor. A U-shape, with the leader sitting at the open end of the U, also works well. With this arrangement, all the children are in front of the leader.

The children enter the Worship Center by walking slowly and quietly, for the opening time is the time children and leaders begin their approach to God. The children are learning that it's time to listen and to become centered on worship. During the approach time we learn the Lord's Prayer, the doxology, the Gloria Patri, and other components of the family worship time, such as praise songs and hymns. Then when the children worship with adults, they can join in on the things they know and will feel more involved.

Since sign language is an effective way of communicating with God and others (and it keeps hands busy and minds involved), we teach the children to sign some of the songs and Bible verses. Two good signing resources are *The Joy of Signing* by Lottie L. Riekhof and *Religious Signing* by Elaine Costello. To simplify things, we sign only the main words of the songs and verses.

The approach to God is followed by the presentation of the Word. To enable the children to see as well as hear the Bible stories, they are told by a leader, using visuals. To tell the stories of Bible characters we use four-inch wooden figures, cloth underlays, and appropriate backgrounds. When we tell stories that Jesus told, we use felt figures on underlays. We use a gold box to store these story materials. This differentiates them from the stories about Bible characters.

After the story is told, the leader and children spend time wondering about the story. This evokes a sense of awe essential to worship and gives the leader and children time to talk about the story. It is the time for the leader to emphasize the truths of the story and to relate the story to experiences the children face.

Sometimes the children are very talkative. Sometimes they are silent and pensive. Both responses are correct. Value the verbal and the silent times. Sometimes the wondering thoughts trigger other thoughts. Follow along as you feel led and as long as the children stay involved. Sometimes I say, "When you have a quiet time, continue thinking about what we have seen and heard today in our Bible story."

After the Word has been presented and talked about, the story and its related materials are placed on the top shelves that surround the room. The stories are arranged in the following order: Old Testament stories, Advent, the nativity, Epiphany, the season of Epiphany, Lent, Easter, the season of Easter, Pentecost, and the season of Pentecost. This helps the children have a sense of the flow of God's Word.

The Worship Center

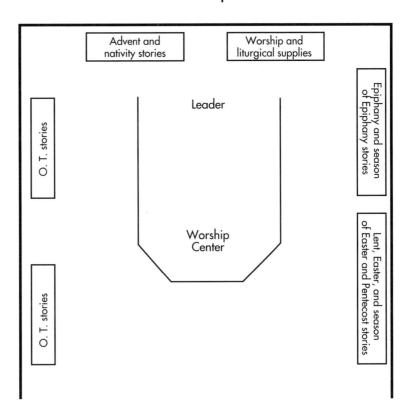

A Worship Center design showing organization of stories on shelves.

Now the children are ready to work with God's stories. They may choose to work with the story-word materials of the story of the day or a previous Bible story. They may want to read a book, work a puzzle, or use a variety of art supplies to draw a picture about a Bible story, to say thank you to God, or tell God something. Crayons, chalk, markers, colored pencils, white paper, colored paper, construction paper, scissors, and glue are all on the bottom shelves around the room. (Art supplies can be concentrated in one area of the room; however, we discovered that there was less congestion when the children were putting things away if the art supplies were spread out on the shelves.) Middle shelves hold the enriching materials such as puzzles, books, activity sheets, and related stories.

Ask the children one by one what each would like to do and dismiss them to begin that activity. If a child does not know what activity to choose, let him sit while you continue around the circle. Sometimes children cannot decide and then it is appropriate to make a suggestion. As a rule, no more than two children should work together.

Before beginning his or her activity, each child should select a carpet piece and place it somewhere in the room. The carpet piece identifies each child's own activity spot.

The children should be taught to be responsible for their Worship Center. Each story is to be handled reverently and put back carefully in its correct place. Be very careful, as a leader, how you handle the Bible story materials and other things in the Worship Center because the children will follow your example. The children should return to the right shelf art supplies, paper, books, and other things they have used. If a child makes something, he or she may take it home.

Sometimes children work on something and do not finish it. A place is needed to keep their work so they can continue the next week. We have been using boxes to make "cubbyholes" for each child. Sturdy boxes with dividers can be picked up from grocery stores and covered with self-adhesive paper. Cubbyholes work well not only for keeping partially completed work, but also for holding toys and purses that inevitably accompany children to the Worship Center. If a child is absent, her take-home paper can be placed in her cubbyhole.

Ring a small bell or dim the lights to let the children know when it is time to put their things away and gather to read the story of the day from the Bible. This emphasizes for the children that the story they saw and heard comes from Scripture. Prayers are offered and a "feast" is celebrated. This feast time helps the children prepare themselves for participation at the Lord's Supper. It may be celebrated weekly, once a month, or as often as you have time.

To conclude the worship time, the children come to the leader for a parting blessing. Each child has a special one-on-one time with the leader who gives him or her an encouraging word, a comforting word, a word of praise, and a parting blessing. Be sure to look the child in the eyes and encourage him or her to look at you.

Leader Preparation

To prepare for leading the children in worship, it is vital that the leader be centered and prepared. Story preparation should begin the Sunday or Monday before the story is to be told so the leader lives with the story for a whole week. Read the Bible passages on which the story is based. Also read

Bible study helps and/or commentaries on the passages during your study time. Read the story from this book, concentrating on the words and actions. Toward the middle of the week practice the story with the figure movements. Do it slowly and reverently, memorizing the actions of the story as you go over it. When the story becomes a part of the leader's life then presenting it to the children is like giving them a personal gift. If the children are restless, it is easy to shorten the story because the study has already been done on it. Conversely, if the children are attentive listeners, it is possible to expand on the story.

Present the stories slowly and reverently with your eyes focused on the story material. Discipline is maintained by drawing the children into God's story. If there are children who wiggle excessively or who are making a disturbance, the adult helper can touch them gently on the shoulder as a reminder to listen quietly. If the disturbance continues, it may be necessary to remove the child from the Worship Center until he or she can behave appropriately. Slow down the telling of the story to help the children pay attention, or stop a moment until everyone is calm and quiet and the atmosphere needed to listen to God's Word returns.

Important Times

Since I began using the children-in-worship ministry, three parts of our worship time have become increasingly powerful and important. They are the two prayer times—before the Bible story is told and during the Bible-reading time—and the final blessing.

Before I tell the Bible story for the day (see the worship outline on page 23), we take a few minutes to be quiet so we can gather the words of God's story. As we sit quietly hugging our knees, we feel God's presence in a powerful way. God is with us; he is present to bless us, to feed us, to empower each of us to be his person. Sometimes God's presence is so real that it is overwhelming, and it takes a few more seconds to refocus on the story and find voice to begin telling the story. The children feel and know this too, because they sit quietly and later verbalize that God was present to them during that time.

When we come back together to read the story from the Bible, the children each pick up a Bible and a Bible marker from the shelf. They find the passage in the Bible and, since

I have older children who can read, we either read it together or take turns reading a verse at a time. The children have made real progress in finding the Bible passages and are able to locate the books in the Bible, as well as chapter and verse. One Sunday one of the boys said, "It sure would have been easier if they had put the Bible together in alphabetical order." It was a good time to explain briefly why the books of the Bible are in the order they are.

After we read the Bible passage, the child helper of the day (whose job it is to set up the Worship Center with the liturgical cloth, candle and holder, Bible, and snuffer) says our prayer for the day. At first the children were hesitant about praying and sometimes asked to be excused. I would then say the prayer, but each time their turn came, I would gently encourage them to verbalize their prayer. Now none of the children hesitate to pray even if guests are present. When it is their turn, they pray. Sometimes the prayers are very short and other times the prayer may include concerns and thanks, but I see great strides in growth in prayer that have taken place over the years we have been together.

The final benediction or blessing at the close of our worship is also a meaningful time. The blessing gives a fit conclusion to our worship. Remember that Jesus modeled the blessing when he took the children in his arms and blessed them (Mark 10:13–16).

As the children come to me one by one, I hold their hands in mine, cup their chin in my hands, or put my arm around them. I look them straight in the eye and give them an encouraging word, a word of comfort, a word of praise, and the blessing. (See the worship outline on page 27.)

Sometimes the child helper of the day gives the blessing. Children can be cruel to each other as they tease and cut each other down, so we thought that helping them see that they could encourage and bless each other was not only possible but also constructive. At first it was hard and they would ask, "But, Mrs. Z., what do I say?" I reminded them of the blessing they receive from me and then they would try. No child ever refused to do it and gradually they became more comfortable and adept at giving the blessing to each other.

Note: Gary Smalley and John Trent share ideas about the parental blessing in their book, *The Blessing,* New York: Pocket Books, 1986.

Blessings from the Bible

Use the following blessings to enrich your own life and then use what you feel is appropriate with the children you lead in worship.

Numbers 6:24–26: The Lord bless you and keep you; the Lord make his face shine upon you and be gracious to you; the Lord turn his face toward you and give you peace.

Romans 16:20: The grace of our Lord Jesus be with you.

2 Corinthians 13:14: May the grace of the Lord Jesus Christ, and the love of God, and the fellowship of the Holy Spirit be with you all.

Ephesians 3:20–21: Now to him who is able to do immeasurably more than all we ask or imagine, according to his power that is at work within us, to him be glory in the church and in Christ Jesus throughout all generations, for ever and ever! Amen.

Ephesians 6:23–24: Peace to the brothers [and sisters], and love with faith from God the Father and the Lord Jesus Christ. Grace to all who love our Lord Jesus Christ with an undying love.

Philippians 4:23: The grace of the Lord Jesus Christ be with your spirit. Amen.

1 Thessalonians 3:12–13: May the Lord make your love increase and overflow for each other and for everyone else. . . . May he strengthen your hearts so that you will be blameless and holy in the presence of our God and Father when our Lord Jesus comes with all his holy ones.

1 Thessalonians 5:28: The grace of our Lord Jesus Christ be with you.

2 Thessalonians 2:16–17: May our Lord Jesus Christ himself and God our Father, who loved us and by his grace gave us eternal encouragement and good hope, encourage your hearts and strengthen you in every good deed and word.

2 Thessalonians 3:16: Now may the Lord of peace himself give you peace at all times and in every way. The Lord be with all of you.

1 Timothy 1:17: Now to the King eternal, immortal, invisible, the only God, be honor and glory for ever and ever. Amen.

2 Timothy 4:22: The Lord be with your spirit. Grace be with you.

Titus 1:4: Grace and peace from God the Father and Christ Jesus our Savior.

Philemon 25: The grace of the Lord Jesus Christ be with your spirit.

Hebrews 13:20–21: May the God of peace, who through the blood of the eternal covenant brought back from the dead our Lord Jesus, that great Shepherd of the sheep, equip you with everything good for doing his will, and may he work in us what is pleasing to him, through Jesus Christ, to whom be glory for ever and ever. Amen.

1 Peter 5:10–11: And the God of all grace, who called you to his eternal glory in Christ, after you have suffered a little while, will himself restore you and make you strong, firm and steadfast. To him be the power for ever and ever. Amen.

2 Peter 1:2: Grace and peace be yours in abundance through the knowledge of God and of Jesus our Lord.

2 Peter 3:18: But grow in the grace and knowledge of our Lord and Savior Jesus Christ. To him be glory both now and forever! Amen.

2 John 3: Grace, mercy and peace from God the Father and from Jesus Christ, the Father's Son, will be with us in truth and love.

Jude 2: Mercy, peace and love be yours in abundance.

Jude 24–25: To him who is able to keep you from falling and to present you before his glorious presence without fault and with great joy—to the only God our Savior be glory, majesty, power and authority, through Jesus Christ our Lord, before all ages, now and forevermore! Amen.

Revelation 22:21: The grace of the Lord Jesus be with God's people. Amen.

Worship Outlines

This section includes a condensed worship outline and an expanded worship outline. Through the condensed worship outline the entire worship approach can be seen at a glance. The expanded worship outline includes the words that the leader says and the actions used every week. In the expanded outline and in all the lessons that follow, the actions or directions are in the narrow left-hand column. The words to say are in the right-hand column.

Condensed Worship Outline

Approach

Entry/Greeting
Call to Worship
Songs of Praise

Word

Prayer: "Be still and know that I am God."
Presentation: (The Bible story for the day)
Personal Meditations: (Children's choices)
Closing Circle:
    Lighting Candle
    Reading Scripture (The Bible passage for the day)
    Prayers

Response

Serving the Feast
Prayers of Thanksgiving
Partaking of the Feast

Blessing

Worship Outline

Approach

Entry/Greeting
Words of greeting: "The Lord be with you."
Response of the children: "And also with you."

Recall with the children that we are here to be with God, to talk with God, and to work with the stories of God.

Call to Worship

Use the words of the Shema with the children for a call to worship.

"Hear, O Israel, the Lord our God is one. And you shall love the Lord your God with all your heart, with all your soul and with all your strength." *(sign)*

Take the offering here. One of the children serves as deacon, collecting the offering, while we all sing the doxology.

Songs of Praise

Word

Prayer: "Be still and know that I am God" *(sign and sing)*

Presentation

This is the signal to the children to sit "hugging their hands" or "hugging their knees" in a manner that will enable them (and allow others) to approach God.

When we sing those words, we know it is time to get ready to hear God's story.

Walk with an air of anticipation to the place on the shelf where the story material is kept. Bring it to the Worship Center.

Watch very carefully where I go so you will always know where these materials can be found. Remember, you may choose to work with this material later, but, for now, hug your hands or your knees, and enjoy the material with your eyes.

Take a moment of silence to focus yourself and the children on God and to gather the words of the story.

Let's take a few moments to be quiet so we can gather the words of God's story.

(The day's Bible story and the wondering time go here.)

Pause, reflect, and then end by showing how to put the materials away with reverence. Use as few words as possible.

Watch what I do with my hands so you will know how to carefully put the materials away when you are finished working with them.

Personal Meditations

Allow the children one by one to choose their work.

I wonder what you would like to do today. You could make something that shows how you feel about today's story (or parable). Perhaps you would like to work with the materials of today's story or of a story we have had before. You may want to look at books or you may have another idea.

Closing Circle

Ring the bell as a signal for the children to put their materials away and gather again in the circle. Light the candle.

[God's] Word is a lamp to my feet and a light for my path (Ps. 119:105).

Look at the Bible for a moment and then gently, lovingly trace the four edges of the Bible with your fingers.

This is the Bible. The story we heard today can be found in the Bible.

Open the Bible to the passage for the day. Read the verses slowly and with feeling.

I will put a marker in this place. This is a picture of _____. *(Fill in the words that come after "Bible marker" included with each week's story.)*

You might like to look at these words in the Bible or have someone read them to you.

Who would like to say a prayer about the story we heard today or about something that is important to you? *(Or have the child helper of the day say the prayer.)*

After the children have prayed, the child helper extinguishes the candle and puts the Bible, candle and holder, snuffer, and cloth back on the shelf.

Response
Serving the Feast

Take a white paper napkin and place it in front of you on the floor. Quietly and carefully, unfold it. Have the child helper distribute napkins to the other children and adults. Have them unfold their napkins. (Paper towels will also work.)

Now it is time for the feast. This is how to make a table for the feast.

Today our feast is _____ *(name the food)*. You may have _____ *(tell the amounts that each may take)*.

Remember to wait until everyone is served and we have prayed before you enjoy our feast.

Have the child or adult helper distribute the food. Have the adult helper distribute the juice. When all the children are served, continue.

Leader: "Let us give thanks to the Lord our God."

Children: "It is right to give thanks and praise."

Prayers of Thanksgiving

Allow sufficient time for praying. Close with your own prayer.

Leader: "Let us pray." *(Encourage every child, adult, and guest to say a "thank you" prayer.)*

Partaking of Feast

Have a joyful time of conversation as you eat. When everyone has finished, gather the four corners of your napkin together. Then put the napkin into the cup, and have the children do the same. The child helper can pass the wastebasket to collect the cups and napkins.

Blessing

Have the children stand and come to you one by one for the blessing. Give each child a good word about his or her involvement in that day's worship experience and the blessing.

Leader: "The love of God goes with you this week. Shalom."

Child: "Shalom."

Part
One

*Old
Testament
Stories*

1

Noah Loves God

Scripture sources: Genesis 6:5–13; Deuteronomy 6:4–9
Materials:
  Figures of Noah, Noah's wife, three children, and
    three adults
  Green underlay
  Tent
  Basket to hold figures
  Tray to hold the materials
Scripture to read: Genesis 6:8–10
Bible marker: A picture of Noah to remind us that
  Noah and his family loved God

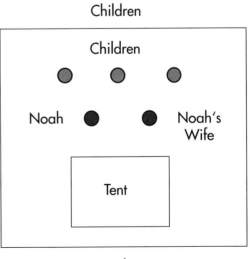

Carefully spread out the green underlay.

A long, long time ago there lived a very special man called Noah.

Present Noah. Set him in the middle of the underlay.

Noah was special because he loved God. Noah was happy that God loved him and took care of him.

Present Noah's wife and set her next to Noah.

Noah and his wife lived in a tent

Present the tent. Set it behind the figures.

Add the children next to the parents.

with their three sons.

Noah and his wife taught their sons to love God. They taught their sons to talk with God in prayer. They taught their sons to say "thank you" to God for their tent home, for their food, for their clothes, and for each other.

Point to Noah and his wife.

Noah and his wife told their sons about God when they woke up in the morning and when they went to bed at night. The family talked with God in prayer at breakfast, lunch, and dinner times. When the boys helped their father during the day, Noah told them again about God. He told them how good God was. Noah told his sons about the gifts God gave them at creation: the gifts of light, water, growing things, sun, moon, stars, birds, fish, animals, and people. Noah told his sons that God cared for them and that God loved them very much. Noah and his wife taught their sons to love God as much as they did.

Pause.

God was happy with Noah.

Pause. With a sweeping motion of the hand, indicate that there are others around Noah's family.

A lot of other people lived around Noah and his family.

Point to Noah.

Noah loved God, so he told other people about God and how good God is. Noah told them about the gifts God gave at creation. Noah told them that God gave them tent homes, food, and clothes and that they should be thankful and love God, too. Noah was kind and helpful to his neighbors all the time.

Shake head "no."

But the other people did not love God as Noah's family did.

Cover your ears with both hands.

They did not listen when Noah told them God loved them and that God wanted them to love God too.

Shake head "no."

They did not want to love and obey God as Noah did. These people just laughed at Noah and his family.

Point to Noah and his family.

But Noah and his family did not care that the people laughed at them. They just continued to love God and did what God wanted them to do. They kept on being kind and helpful to others. And God kept taking care of them.

One by one, exchange a child figure with an adult figure.

Noah's sons grew and grew until they became grown-up men who, like their father, loved God.

Point to each figure in turn.

Noah's sons were named Shem, Ham, and Japheth. Noah and his wife loved God. Shem, Ham, and Japheth loved God too. They also pleased God.

Pause and reflect on the whole scene.

Begin the wondering time.

I wonder what it was like living in a tent home.

Noah helped the people who lived around him. I wonder what he did to help them.

I wonder if other people have helped you.

I wonder what we can do to help others.

You may want to write the children's ideas down on a twelve-inch-wide, six-foot-long piece of newsprint. When finished, tape the ends of the paper to empty paper towel rolls, roll up from each end like a scroll and tie with yarn. Review these ideas over the summer and remind the children to keep helping others.

I wonder if we can tell others about God like Noah did.

Return to the worship outline and continue.

2

Noah Obeys God

Scripture source: Genesis 6
Materials:
    Figures, underlay, and tray from previous story
    Ark
    Pictures or plastic models (or the real thing) of grain,
       grass, wheat, bread, fruits, and vegetables
    Basket to hold food
Scripture to read: Genesis 6:14–16, 22
Bible marker: A picture of Noah building the big boat
    called an ark to remind us that Noah obeyed God

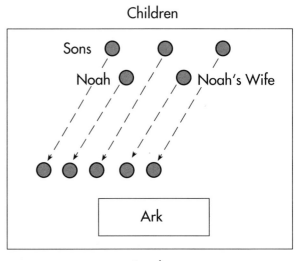

Children

Leader

Carefully spread out the underlay. Place Noah, his wife, and their three sons on the underlay.

Noah, his wife, and their three sons—Shem, Ham, and Japheth—loved God very much. They also obeyed God and did what God told them to do.

Indicate with a sweeping motion of your hand the people around Noah's family. Shake your head "no."

The people around Noah did not love God.

Cover your ears with both hands.

They would not listen when Noah told them about God. The people just kept on being mean and cruel and wicked.

Point to each figure in turn.

But Noah and his wife loved God and told their boys about God. They told their boys about God in the morning, while they worked, and before they went to sleep at night. They also talked with God in prayer.

Point to Noah.

Now one day God told Noah to build a very big boat. God was going to make it rain and rain. God was going to wash his world so it would be all clean and new again as it was at the beginning. But God wanted to keep Noah and his family safe because they loved God and obeyed him.

So God told Noah to build a very, very, very big boat called an ark. The boat had to be very big because it had to hold a lot of animals, Noah and his family, and all the food they would need while it rained.

Move Noah away from the rest of the figures.

Noah listened to God. Noah listened very carefully as God told him just how to build the ark. God told Noah what kind of wood to use. God told Noah to make rooms in the ark. God told Noah to cover all the cracks inside and outside the ark so no water could get in. God told Noah to make it three stories high and to put a roof on top. God told Noah to make a door in the side of the ark.

Point to Noah.

Noah listened very carefully to all God told him. Then Noah obeyed God. He went right to work. He sharpened his tools, chopped down trees, sawed them into boards, and put the boards together.

Move the three sons next to Noah.

When Noah's sons were old enough they helped their father. They worked and worked for many long days, weeks, months, and even years. The boat grew bigger and bigger. They built it just as God said, with rooms inside and three stories high. They put a big door on the side so their family and all the animals could get in.

Add the ark without a roof to the scene. The ark was almost finished but it needed a roof. So Noah and his sons worked even harder and made a roof big enough to cover the whole ark.

Add the roof. Finally the great ark was built. But Noah and his sons had to make sure no water leaked in so they filled all the cracks between the boards. Now Noah and his family needed to gather food. Noah, his family, and the animals needed food to eat while they were in the ark. So Noah and his family gathered grass and grain for the animals.

Present stalks of grain. Place them on the underlay near the ark. Present the other food. Place near the ark. They gathered wheat so they could make bread. They gathered dates, raisins, and figs, and onions and other vegetables. They needed a lot of food to feed their family and all the animals. Finally everything was ready.

Point to the ark. The ark was all built.

Point to the food. The food was all stored on board.

Pause and reflect on the whole scene.

Begin the wondering time.

I wonder how Noah felt as he built the big boat.

I wonder how Noah's sons felt as they helped their father.

I wonder what food Noah had to put in the ark.

Talk about how Noah obeyed God.

I wonder how we can obey God.

Return to the worship outline and continue.

3

Two by Two

Scripture source: Genesis 6–7
Materials:
  Figures, underlay, ark, and tray from previous story
  Figures of any number of pairs of animals and three
    women
Scripture to read: Genesis 6:18–21; 7:13, 16–18
Bible marker: A picture of the animals entering the ark
  to remind us of how God kept them and Noah's family
  safe

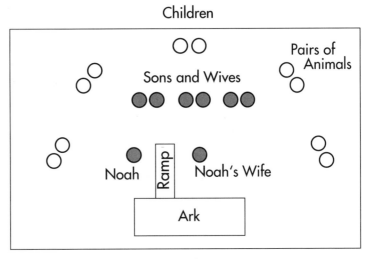

Carefully spread out the underlay. Present Noah and his family. Set them on the middle of the underlay.

Noah, his wife, and their boys obeyed God. They loved God and listened to God.

Add the ark behind the figures. Put the ramp (the removable roof piece) against the ark.

Noah listened to God and built a very, very, very big boat called an ark. Now the ark was all ready.

Put the food into the ark.

Noah and his family put all the food into the ark—the grass and grain for the animals, the fruit and vegetables for the people.

Add the three women figures.

By this time Noah's sons had married. They and their wives were ready to enter the ark. God said to Noah, "Come in. Come into the ark, you and your family. After seven days, I will make it rain for a long, long time." So Noah and his family walked up, up, up the ramp.

Move a son and his wife into the ark.

Shem and his wife went into the ark.

Move a second son and wife into the ark.

Ham and his wife went into the ark.

Move the third son and wife into the ark.

Japheth and his wife went into the ark.

Move Noah and his wife toward the ark. Leave Noah at the bottom of the ramp. Move Noah's wife inside.

After Noah's family was settled in the ark, God sent the animals and birds to him. Two by two they came.

Present the animals. Place them in a semicircle on the underlay facing the ark.

A father and mother of every kind of animal and bird came to the ark. There were large animals, medium-sized animals, and little animals. There were also birds in pairs.

Continue adding pairs of animals until you feel you have enough. Then move them into the ark. When all are in, move Noah inside.

At last all the animals, birds, and people were inside the ark, the great big boat.

Close the ark by replacing the ramp board on the roof.

Then a most wonderful thing happened! God shut the door tight! God closed the door of the ark. Now Noah, his wife, and their family; all the birds; and all the animals were safe! No one could open the door, and no rain would fall on them.

Pause.

Noah had obeyed God. Noah had done just what God had told him to do. Noah knew God would keep them safe.

Pause and reflect on the whole scene.

Begin the wondering time.

I wonder how it felt to have the ark all built.

I wonder how long it took to store the food on the ark.

I wonder what Noah and his family had to do on the ark to care for all the animals.

I wonder what it was like to live on the ark with all the animals.

I wonder if you can name some of the animals that entered the ark.

Return to the worship outline and continue.

4

Noah Is Safe

Scripture sources: Genesis 7–8; 2 Peter 2:5; 3:3–7; Matthew 24:37–39

Materials:
  Figures, underlay, ark, and tray from previous story
  Figure of a dove
  Olive leaf made of felt

Scripture to read: Genesis 7:17–18; 8:1, 4, 8–12

Bible marker: A picture of the ark in the rain to remind us that God kept Noah, his family, the animals, and the birds safe inside it

Children

Ark

Leader

Carefully spread out the underlay. Have the animals and Noah and his family in the ark. Present the ark and set it on the underlay. Review the story with the children. Remind them of:

1. Noah's love for God

2. Noah's obedience

3. Safety in the ark

The people, animals, and birds were in the ark, the big boat. They waited for the rain to come.

Pause.

And then they heard it! The rain started! They heard the rain hit the roof!

With your fingers wiggling (to indicate rain), bring your hands down over the ark. Do this several times.

It rained and it rained and it rained. Harder and harder the rain fell. The streams filled up, the rivers filled up, and still it rained! The water rose higher and higher.

Place your hands, palms up, under the ark so as you say "and higher and higher" you can lift the ark up into the air.

It came up the sides of the ark until the big boat moved! The ark was floating!

Move the ark back and forth.

Back and forth the big boat floated on the water. Still more rain kept falling until the hills and then the mountains were covered. It rained for forty days and forty nights.

But Noah, his family, the birds, and animals were safe and snug and warm inside the ark. They had plenty of food to eat. Noah had obeyed God and now they were safe.

Slowly bring the ark down.

Finally the rain stopped. Noah and his family woke up one morning and listened. No rain! "It's stopped raining," Noah said to his family. "The rain has stopped!"

Noah and his family waited and waited. It would take a long time for so much water to go away. God remembered Noah and his family and sent a strong wind to help dry up the water.

Set the ark on the underlay.

Finally the ark rested on a mountaintop. It no longer floated on the water. But that didn't mean all the water was gone. There was still a lot of water everywhere. Noah and his family waited and waited. Noah wondered how far the water had gone down, so he decided on a plan. He would send out a dove.

Present the dove. Transfer the dove to the other hand and move it in a wide circle. Transfer the dove to the first hand, closing it and drawing it next to you.

The dove flew back and forth over the water, but it could find no tree to sit on. She flew back to Noah who took her back into the ark. After seven days, Noah sent the dove out again.

Repeat the previous motions, only this time, after the dove returns, place a green leaf with the dove on your open hand.

This time the dove brought back an olive leaf. Noah and his family knew the waters were almost gone.

Present the dove. Repeat the previous motions only this time return the dove to the basket.

After seven days, Noah sent the dove out again. This time the dove did not come back. Now Noah knew the ground was dry! The waters were all gone! But Noah waited until God told him it was okay to leave the ark.

Pause and reflect on the whole scene.

Begin the wondering time.

I wonder how Noah and his family felt when they heard the rain fall.

I wonder what Noah and his family did everyday in the ark.

I wonder if it was hard to wait for the rain to stop and the water to dry up.

I wonder what Noah and hs family thought when the dove came back.

I wonder what Noah and his family thought when the dove brought a leaf back.

I wonder what Noah and his family thought when the dove didn't come back.

I wonder how much longer Noah and his family needed to wait before God opened the door.

Return to the worship outline and continue.

5

Noah Thanks God

Scripture source: Genesis 8; 9:1–17

Materials:

   Figures, underlay, ark, and tray from previous story

   Rainbow sun-catcher

   Stones for the altar

Scripture to read: Genesis 8:15–19; 9:12–16

Bible marker: A picture of Noah and the rainbow to remind us of God's promise to never again send so much rain

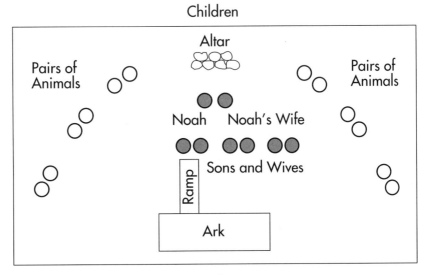

Carefully spread out the underlay. Have the animals and Noah and his family in the ark. Present the ark and set it on the underlay. Review the story with the children. Remind them of:

1. Noah's love for God

2. Noah's obedience

3. Safety in the ark

Set up the ramp and slowly move the pairs out of the ark. Set the animals in pairs in a semicircle facing outward. Set Noah and his family in the middle of the semicircle.

Point to Noah.

Present the stones.

Make an altar. Point to Noah.

Point to Noah's wife.

Point to each son and wife in turn.

Now God said to Noah, "Come out of the ark, you and your wife, your sons and their wives, and all the animals."

Noah and his family were very glad to be safe and on dry ground again. They were very thankful that God had kept them safe.

Noah wanted to show God how thankful he was that God had taken such good care of him and his family.

Noah found some big stones and piled them up to make an altar.

Noah knelt down and said, "Thank you, God, for taking care of us."

Noah's wife said, "Thank you, God."

Shem and his wife said, "Thank you, God." Ham and his wife said, "Thank you, God." Japheth and his wife said, "Thank you, God. Thank you, God, for taking such good care of us and for taking care of the birds and animals and for bringing us safely back to dry ground." God was pleased to hear them say "thank you." God said to Noah, "I promise you that I will never again send such a big flood to cover everything. I will send rain but not so much that it covers the whole world."

Present the rainbow.   "Do you see my beautiful rainbow in the sky? Whenever you see my beautiful rainbow, you will remember my promise to you."

Point to Noah and his family.   Noah and his family looked up into the sky, and there was a beautiful rainbow—red, orange, yellow, green, blue, and purple. After that, whenever Noah and his family saw a rainbow in the sky, they remembered God's promise. God also promised to send seedtime and harvest, cold and heat, summer and winter, day and night in order, for as long as the world lasts. Now when we see the rainbow, we can remember God's promise that he will never again send a big flood to cover the whole earth.

Pause.   God cared for Noah and kept him safe. God cares for us too, and when we see the rainbow, we can remember that God loves and cares for us.

Pause and reflect on the whole scene.

Begin the wondering time.

I wonder how Noah and his family felt as they finally left the ark.

I wonder how the animals felt to finally leave the ark.

I wonder if you have seen a rainbow.

What does it remind us of?

God cared for Noah and kept him safe. I wonder how we can thank God for taking care of us every day.

You might want to take a few minutes to have the children thank God for his care for us.

Return to the worship outline and continue.

6

God Destroys Sodom

Scripture source: Genesis 13:1–13; 18; 19:1–29
Materials:
  Figures of Abraham, three visitors, Lot, Lot's wife,
    and Lot's two daughters
  Green underlay
  Orange felt flames
  Inside of a house background
  City of Sodom background
  Basket to hold figures
Scripture to read: Genesis 18:32–33; 19:1–3, 16–17,
  23–29
Bible marker: A picture of Abraham's three visitors
  who told him God was going to destroy the wicked
  city of Sodom

Children

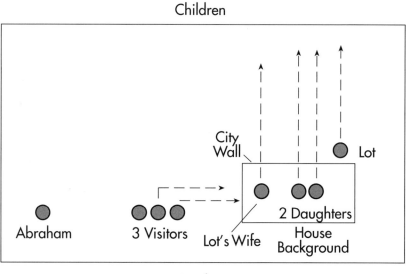

Leader

Carefully spread out the underlay. Add Abraham. Set him on the left near the corner of the underlay.

Present the three men. Set them next to Abraham.

Three men visited Abraham and told him that he and Sarah would have a son.

They also came with sad news about the city of Sodom.

Set the house background on the right of the underlay. Set the city background in front of the house background. Point to one of the figures.

One of the visitors told Abraham that Sodom was so wicked that God was going to destroy it.

Point to Abraham.

But Abraham pleaded with the visitors. "What if there are ten righteous people in Sodom? Will you destroy the ten righteous people?"

The visitor agreed to spare the city if there were ten righteous people.

Remove Abraham and one visitor. Present Lot.

Lot, Abraham's nephew, lived in the city of Sodom. Lot had come from Ur to the Promised Land with Abraham and Sarah. Abraham lived in the hills, but Lot had chosen to live in the city.

Set Lot in front of the city.

Cities in those days had high, thick, stone walls with doors called gates where the people and animals could come in and go out. At night the gates were closed for safety. In the morning the gates were opened for the day for all to come and go. Now this evening, just before the gates were to be closed, Lot was sitting in the gateway.

Move the two visitors toward the city.

Lot saw the two visitors coming.

Move Lot to meet the two and have him bow.

He got up, went to meet them, and bowed with his face to the ground before them. Lot said, "Please come to my home. You can wash your feet, spend the night, and be on your way in the morning." At first the visitors refused. "We'll just sleep in the city park," they said. But Lot insisted.

After their supper the visitors told Lot the sad news about Sodom. "God has seen how wicked the city of Sodom has become. God is going to destroy this city so get your relatives and leave."

When morning came, the visitors hurried Lot, saying, "Quick, take your wife and two daughters and get out!"

"Hurry or you will be destroyed with the city."

But Lot didn't seem to understand. He did not hurry, so the visitors grabbed him by the hand.

They led Lot, his wife, and his two daughters out of the city. The visitors said, "Now run for your lives. Don't look back. Don't stop anywhere until you get to the mountains or you will be destroyed too!"

But Lot protested, "Oh, no! Please don't send me to the mountains! I am afraid of the mountains. See there is a little village close by."

"Please, please, let me go to that little village. It's really small. I'll be safe there."

The visitors would not argue with Lot anymore. "Okay," they replied. "We won't destroy the little village. But hurry! We cannot destroy Sodom until you are safe."

So Lot, his wife, and their two daughters hurried to the little village.

Then God sent fire and flaming sulfur down on Sodom, on a nearby city called Gomorrah, and on all the other cities around them except the little village to which Lot and his family had fled.

God completely destroyed Sodom and Gomorrah because the people were so wicked.

Point to Lot's wife. Lot's wife didn't obey God. The visitors had told them not to look back, but Lot's wife looked back.

Turn the wife to look at the city. When she did, Lot's wife became a block of salt.

Add Abraham to the scene. Set him where he was at the beginning. In the morning Abraham looked toward Sodom and saw the smoke rising toward the sky.

Indicate the city. God kept his promise and destroyed the cities because they were so wicked.

Point to Lot. But God kept Lot safe.

Pause and reflect on the whole scene.

Begin the wondering time.

I wonder why Lot chose to live in the city.

I wonder why Lot was kind to the two visitors.

I wonder how Lot and his family felt when the visitors told them to leave their home.

I wonder how Lot and his family felt as they fled from their home to the little village.

I wonder why Lot's wife looked back.

I wonder how Lot and his daughters felt when their home was destroyed.

I wonder how Abraham felt when he saw the smoke of the cities and knew there were not even ten righteous people.

Return to the worship outline and continue.

7

Isaac and Rebekah

Scripture source: Genesis 21:1–7; 24

Materials:

 Figures of Abraham, Isaac, Rebekah, servant, and two
   camels

   Green underlay

   Well and jar

   Basket to hold materials

Scripture to read: Genesis 24:1–4, 61–67

Bible marker: A picture of Isaac and Rebekah to remind us of how God helped them become husband
   and wife

Children

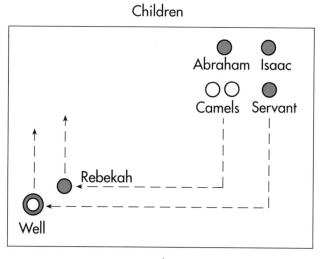

Leader

Carefully spread out the green underlay. Present Isaac.	Isaac, Abraham's son, grew from a baby to a boy to a man.
Set Isaac on the far right corner of the underlay. Present Abraham.	He helped his father Abraham take care of the animals. They had many sheep, cattle, camels, and goats to care for.
Set Abraham next to Isaac.	God had blessed Abraham. But Abraham was getting old and would soon die. He wanted Isaac to have a wife before he died. He wanted a wife from his own people, the ones he had left to come to the Promised Land.
Present the servant.	So Abraham called his servant and told him, "Go back to my people and find a wife for my son Isaac."
Set the servant next to Abraham.	"God will guide you to the right woman," Abraham added.
Present the camels.	So the servant made the preparations for the long trip. He loaded the camels with food. He also took beautiful presents.
Move the camels and servant along the right edge to the near right corner and then along the near edge to the left corner of the underlay.	It took the servant and camels a long time to travel. Finally, many days later as the sun was setting, they arrived at the city and stopped near a well of water.
Add the well to the scene.	It was the custom in that day that at evening, when it was cool, the women would come to the well to fill their water jars.
Point to the servant.	The servant prayed, "Please, God, help me find the right woman to be Isaac's wife."
Pause.	The servant continued, "I am next to a well. I will ask one of the women for a drink and if she says, 'Yes,' and then offers to water my camels, too, then I will know that she is the one you have chosen for Isaac."
Present Rebekah.	As the servant finished praying, the women came to fill their big jars with water.
Set Rebekah next to the servant. Present the jar and set it next to Rebekah.	One of them was called Rebekah.

Point to the servant.   The servant asked Rebekah, "May I, please, have a drink?"

Point to Rebekah.   "Oh, yes," she replied giving him a drink. Then she added, "I'll water your camels, too."

Point to the servant.   The servant quietly watched her as she poured water into the trough so the camels could drink.

Move the servant, Rebekah, and the camels a short way up the left edge.   The servant and Rebekah went to Rebekah's home where the servant explained to Rebekah and her family why he had come.

Point to the servant.   The servant said, "I work for Abraham, your relative. God has blessed Abraham. He is very wealthy and has many sheep, cattle, camels, and donkeys. Abraham sent me here to find a wife for his son, Isaac. When I came to the well of water, I asked God to show me the right woman. She would be the one who would give me a drink and then offer to give my camels a drink too. Rebekah did that. She gave me a drink and then gave my camels a drink. I thank God for answering my prayer so quickly. Now, can Rebekah come with me and be Isaac's wife?"

Rebekah's father and brother listened carefully and then said, "This is what God wants. Rebekah may go with you if she wishes."

Point to Rebekah.   Rebekah replied, "I will go with you. I will become Isaac's wife."

Point to the servant.   The servant gave the presents he had brought—gold and silver jewelry and fine clothes—to Rebekah and her family. In the morning the servant and Rebekah left to go back to the Promised Land where Abraham and Isaac lived.

Slowly move the camels, servant, and Rebekah back along the path the servant had traveled before.   Slowly the camels carried them to the land God had promised to give to Abraham and his children and his children's children.

Point to Isaac.   One day as Isaac was in the field, he noticed the camels in the distance.

Have the camels, servant, and Rebekah arrive next to Isaac.   When the servant, Rebekah, and the camels got to Isaac, the servant explained everything that had happened.

Move Isaac and Rebekah next to each other.

Isaac and Rebekah were married and loved each other very much.

Point to each figure in turn.

God answered the prayers of Abraham, Isaac, and the servant. God had helped the servant find a wife for Isaac.

Pause and reflect on the whole scene.

Begin the wondering time.

I wonder what it was like for the servant to go and find a wife for Isaac.

I wonder what he was thinking as he traveled.

I wonder what Rebekah and her family thought when the servant told them the purpose of his journey.

I wonder how Isaac felt when the servant brought back beautiful Rebekah to be his wife.

Talk about how God answered Abraham's, Isaac's, and the servant's prayers.

Talk about what we can ask for when we talk with God in prayer.

Talk about how God answers our prayers.

Return to the worship outline and continue.

8

Esau and Jacob

Scripture source: Genesis 25:19–28:9
Materials:
  Figures of Isaac, Rebekah, Esau, and Jacob
  Green underlay
  Tent
  Stones for an altar
  Basket to hold figures
  Tray to hold materials
Scripture to read: Genesis 25:24–28; 27:41–45
Bible marker: A picture of Isaac and Rebekah and their
  twin sons to remind us of the blessing God promised
  Isaac

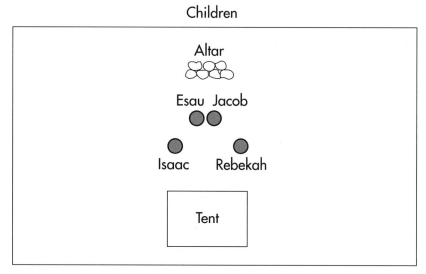

Children

Altar

Esau Jacob

Isaac   Rebekah

Tent

Leader

Carefully spread out the green underlay.	God led Abraham's servant to Rebekah and she became Isaac's wife.
Present Isaac and Rebekah.	Isaac and Rebekah were very happy together.
Set them on the right side of the underlay. Add the tent.	They lived in a tent. Rebekah prepared the food and made the clothes, while Isaac cared for the sheep, cattle, camels, and goats. Isaac was very wealthy and had much to care for.
Point to Isaac.	Isaac was a peace-loving man. If others quarreled over wells of water or filled the wells with dirt, Isaac moved to a different place. He did not want to argue or quarrel with anyone.
	One night God appeared to Isaac and said, "I am the God of your father Abraham. Do not be afraid. I will bless you as I blessed Abraham." Isaac was happy to know God was with him.
Add the stones to the scene.	He built an altar to say "thank you" to God for being with him as God was with his father Abraham.
Pause. Point to Isaac and Rebekah.	Now Isaac and Rebekah were getting older and still they had no children. So Isaac prayed to God and asked for a child. God heard Isaac's prayer. God sent not one child but two! Twin boys were born to Isaac and Rebekah. The firstborn son was named Esau and the secondborn was named Jacob.
Add Esau to the scene.	Even though Esau and Jacob were twins, they were very different. Esau was hairy and red-faced. He was strong and lively and he liked to go hunting. Esau would take his bow and arrow and hunt wild animals. Isaac, his father, liked the taste of the wild animals that Esau brought home and cooked, so Isaac loved Esau best.
Add Jacob to the scene.	Jacob was quiet and thoughtful. He liked to stay at home and care for the sheep. Rebekah loved Jacob best.
Pause.	The boys grew to be men. In that day, when a father died, the firstborn son received twice as much of what the father owned as the other sons did. This was called his "birthright," because it was his right as the firstborn.

Point to Esau.	So Esau, as the firstborn, had the "birthright" to more of what Isaac owned and also the "right" to God's blessing as the leader of the family. But Esau did not care about his "birthright" or the blessing.
Move Esau away from the others.	One day Esau took his bow and arrow and went to hunt some animals. He traveled far and wide, scrambling over rocks and down into valleys looking for wild animals to make into the stew he knew his father loved.
Turn Esau back toward home.	But Esau found nothing. After hunting all day, he turned toward home, tired and disappointed.
Point to Jacob.	While Esau was away hunting, Jacob stayed home and made a pot of lentil stew. It was a delicious, hearty soup.
Move Esau back to where Jacob is.	When Esau returned, he smelled the stew. "Give me some of your stew," he said to his brother. "I am famished!"
Point to Jacob.	"I'll trade you some stew for your birthright," said Jacob.
Point to Esau.	"What good is my birthright, when I'm starving?" said Esau. "It's a deal!"
Point to Jacob.	"Promise me before God that you mean it," said Jacob.
Point to Esau.	So Esau promised. Jacob gave Esau the stew and Esau ate it. Then he went on as though nothing had happened. He never told his father what he had done.
Pause. Point to Isaac.	Isaac grew old and feeble. His eyesight became so bad that he was nearly blind. One day he said to Esau, "Get some wild game. Make me the stew you know I like and then I'll give you the family blessing." So Esau left.
Move Esau to where he was before when he went hunting. Point to Rebekah.	Rebekah heard what Isaac said. She called Jacob. "Make some stew for your father and then go to him to get the blessing," she said.
Point to Jacob.	"But," said Jacob, "Father will know it's me and not Esau. His skin is hairy; mine is smooth. Father will curse me instead of blessing me."
Point to Rebekah.	Rebekah replied, "Leave that to me. Go, get two small goats."
Point to Jacob.	Jacob did as his mother said. Rebekah took the skins of the goats and put them on Jacob's arms and neck. She had Jacob wear Esau's clothes and take the stew to Isaac.

Move Jacob next to Isaac. Point to Isaac.

Isaac asked, "Are you my son, Esau?" Jacob lied, "Yes, I am." Isaac said, "Let me feel your skin. You feel and smell like Esau but you sound like Jacob." Isaac ate the stew and then gave the family blessing to Jacob.

Move Jacob away from his father. Move Esau back home and next to his father.

Soon afterward Esau returned home. He made some stew and brought it in to his father. "Father," he said, "here is your stew. Eat it and bless me."

Point to Isaac.

Isaac trembled. "Who are you?" he asked. "I just ate some stew and gave the blessing!"

Point to Esau.

Esau began to cry bitterly. "My brother has tricked me. He took my birthright and now he has taken my blessing. Father, bless me, too."

Point to Isaac.

Isaac said, "Your brother has received the family blessing. He will rule over you. But some day you shall shake off your brother's rule and be free."

Move Esau away from Isaac.

Esau left his father. He was very angry and said, "My father is old. After he dies, I'll get even with my brother."

Pause and reflect on the whole scene.

Begin the wondering time.

I wonder how Isaac and Rebekah felt when they had no children.

I wonder who remembers who else was old and still had no children.

I wonder how they felt when twin sons were born to them.

I wonder why Isaac loved Esau best and Rebekah loved Jacob best.

I wonder how the boys felt about that.

I wonder why Esau thought so little of his birthright.

I wonder why he sold it so easily.

I wonder how Jacob felt when he was lying to his father.

I wonder how Esau felt when he knew Jacob had taken his blessing.

I wonder what will happen next to Jacob and Esau.

Return to the worship outline and continue.

9

Jacob's Dream

Scripture source: Genesis 27:41–33:20; 35

Materials:

    Figures of Jacob, Esau, Laban, Leah, Rachel, four children, and six sheep

    Green underlay

    Stairs, angels, veil, and well

    Stone for the pillow

    Stones for an altar

    Basket to hold figures

    Tray to hold all materials

Scripture to read: Genesis 28:10–22; 35:9–15

Bible marker: A picture of Jacob and the ladder with angels going up and down to remind us of Jacob's dream, the blessing God gave him, and the promise he made to God

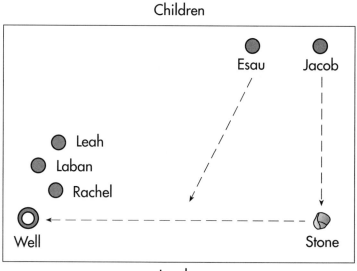

Carefully spread out the green underlay. Present Jacob.

Jacob bought his brother's birthright for a pot of stew. He received the family blessing by deceiving his father.

Set Jacob on the far right corner. Present Esau.

Esau, the older brother, was angry. He sold his birthright, and now Jacob had received the family blessing. Esau said, "My father is old and cannot live long. When he is dead, I will kill my brother Jacob because of what he has done." Rebekah heard about this. She called Jacob and said "Leave home. Go to my brother Laban. Maybe if Esau doesn't see you for awhile, he'll forget. I'll send for you later."

Set Esau next to Jacob. Begin moving Jacob to the near right corner. (Jacob should be moved along the same route the servant used in the "Isaac and Rebekah" story.)

So Jacob left to go to his uncle Laban's home, the place where his mother had come from many years before.

Continue moving Jacob until he gets to the near right corner.

Jacob left home by himself. He walked and walked. One evening, just about sunset, he came to a place in the mountains. Since Jacob had no bed, he took a stone for a pillow

Present the stone. Lay it on the near right corner and have Jacob lie down placing his head on the stone.

and rested his head on it. He fell asleep. That night Jacob had a dream.

Present the stairs.

In his dream, Jacob saw stairs leading from the earth up to heaven. Angels were going up and coming down the stairs.

Add the angels to the stairs.

At the top of the stairs, Jacob saw the Lord God. God said, "I am the Lord, the God of Abraham, the God of Isaac your father, and I am your God. The land where you are lying shall belong to you and to your children after you. Your children will spread over the whole land, to the east and west, to the north and south, like the dust of the earth. All peoples on earth will be blessed through you. I am with you. I will keep you. I will bring you back to this land. I will never leave you, and I will surely keep my promise to you."

Remove angels and stairs. Set Jacob upright.

When Jacob awoke, he said, "Surely the presence of the Lord is in this place and I didn't know it. I thought I was all alone, but God is with me. This is the house of God; it is the gate of heaven."

Set the stone on end, upright.

Jacob took the stone he had used as a pillow and set it upright.

With one hand, use a pouring motion over the stone.

Then he poured oil on it as an offering to God. Jacob made a promise to God, saying, "If God really goes with me and keeps me and gives me bread to eat and brings me back to my father's house in peace, then the Lord will be my God." Jacob made a further promise. "Of all that God gives me, I will give one tenth, a tithe, back to God."

Move Jacob along the near edge to the left corner.

Jacob continued his journey.

Add the well to the near left corner.

Finally, he came to the well outside of the city. Maybe it was the same well the servant had come to, where he found Jacob's mother, Rebekah.

Present Rachel. Set her next to the well.

Rachel was there to water the sheep. Jacob helped her. He found out she was his uncle Laban's daughter. Rachel was beautiful and Jacob was already falling in love with her. Jacob went home with Rachel and met her father, Laban.

Add Laban to the scene. Remove Rachel.

He worked for Laban for a month. Then Laban said, "I know you are my sister's son, but you don't need to work for nothing. I'll pay you."

Point to Jacob.

Jacob loved Rachel so he said, "I'll work for you for seven years in return for your younger daughter Rachel."

Point to Laban.

This seemed good to Laban, so he agreed.

Point to Jacob.

Jacob loved Rachel so much that the seven years went by very fast. The day of the wedding finally came.

Add Leah covered with a veil.

In came the bride covered with a thick veil as was the custom of that day. After the wedding, when Jacob lifted the veil, he discovered that the bride was Leah, Rachel's older sister, not Rachel, the one he loved.

Remove the veil.

Laban had tricked Jacob.

Point to Jacob.	Jacob was angry.
Point to Laban.	"But," said Laban, "in our land we can't let the younger daughter get married before her older sister. Keep Leah. Work seven more years and you can have Rachel too." In those days, sometimes men had more than one wife. So Jacob worked for seven more years for Rachel.
Return Rachel to the scene.	Then Jacob and Rachel were married.
Add children to the scene.	Jacob had many children. He worked for Laban twenty years in all and became very wealthy.
Add the sheep.	Then one day Jacob decided to go back home.
Begin moving Jacob, Leah, Rachel, the children, and the sheep, back along the route Jacob took. Laban will stay on the underlay on the left side.	Everyone had to move slowly because of the children and animals.
Begin moving Esau to meet Jacob just before Jacob gets to the stone.	Jacob was afraid to meet his brother. Was Esau still angry? Would Esau remember his promise to kill him? So Jacob sent a present to Esau.
Move half of the sheep ahead.	He sent many sheep, cattle, camels, and goats. Maybe Esau would forgive him if the present were large enough.
Have Esau and Jacob meet.	When the brothers finally met, Esau and Jacob kissed each other and cried.
Have Esau stay where they met. Move Jacob and the rest to the near right corner.	Jacob, Leah, Rachel, and the children continued their journey and finally arrived at the place where, a long time ago, God had talked with Jacob in a dream.
Point to the stone.	Now God talked with Jacob again. God said, "Your name is no longer Jacob but Israel. I am God Almighty. The land I gave to Abraham and Isaac, I give to you and to your children after you. I am the Lord God. I will bless you and make you great. You are blessed to be a blessing."

Add the altar stones. Jacob, now called Israel, built an altar to say "thank you" to God for being with him on his journey and bringing him safely back home.

Pause and reflect on the whole scene.

Begin the wondering time.

I wonder how Jacob felt as he left home.

I wonder what he thought about as he walked.

I wonder how Jacob felt when Laban tricked him.

I wonder if Jacob remembered how he had tricked his brother and father.

I wonder how Jacob felt as he worked for Laban.

I wonder how Jacob felt as he journeyed back to his home.

I wonder what Esau was thinking as he came to meet Jacob.

I wonder what Jacob was thinking as Esau was coming to meet him.

I wonder how Jacob felt as he listened to God again.

Return to the worship outline and continue.

10

Burning Bush

Scripture sources: Exodus 2:11–4:30; Mark 12:26;
  Luke 20:37–38; Acts 7:23–35; Hebrews 11:24–25
Materials:
  Figures of Moses, Jethro, Zipporah, and three sheep
  Sand-colored underlay
  Burning bush, well, and shepherd's staff
  Basket to hold materials
Scripture to read: Exodus 3:1–10
Bible marker: A picture of Moses standing before a
  burning bush to remind us of how God called Moses
  to lead his people out of Egypt

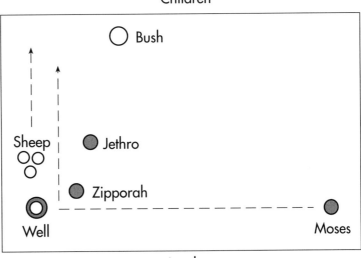

Carefully spread out the underlay. Present Moses and hold him as you say:

Moses grew from a baby, to a boy, to a man. He went to school in the palace; he knew all the wisdom of Egypt. But Moses was still one of God's people.

Place Moses on the right corner of the underlay.

One day when Moses was forty years old, he went to see his own people who had to work very hard for the Pharaoh, the ruler of Egypt. Moses saw one of God's people being beaten by an Egyptian.

Turn your head from side to side as though looking.

Moses quickly looked from side to side and seeing no one, he killed the Egyptian and buried the body in the sand. But the murder was discovered, so Moses had to flee, to run far away.

Move Moses along the edge of the underlay to the left corner.

After a long, long walk, Moses came to the land of Midian.

Add the well next to Moses.

Moses was tired and thirsty, so he sat on the edge of a well to rest.

Add Zipporah and the sheep to the scene.

Now seven sisters came to the well to draw water for their sheep. But some rough shepherds also came and drove the sisters and their sheep away.

Point to Moses.

Moses watched what was happening. When he saw the rough shepherds being mean to the sisters, he got up and drove the rough shepherds away. Moses even drew water from the well and watered the sisters' sheep.

Move the sheep and Zipporah along the left edge of the underlay slightly away from the well. Present Jethro and hold him as you say:

When the sisters returned home, their father was surprised. "Why have you come back so soon?" he asked.

Place Jethro next to the sheep.

The sisters replied, "An Egyptian helped us. He drove the rough shepherds away and even drew water from the well for our sheep." Jethro said, "Well, where is this Egyptian? Go, get him, and invite him to have something to eat!"

Move Moses from the well next to Jethro.	The sisters went to get Moses. Moses not only ate a meal with Jethro and the sisters but he stayed with them for forty years.
Move the sheep by Moses.	During those forty years Moses took care of Jethro's sheep.
Slowly move the sheep and Moses along the left edge until they are in the far corner.	Midian was a desert country so not much rain fell and not much grass grew. Moses had to go long distances to find something for the sheep to eat.
Present and add the burning bush setting it a short distance from Moses.	Now one day as Moses was tending the sheep, he saw a bush burning. As he watched, he noticed that the bush did not burn up but just kept burning.
Point to Moses.	*That is strange,* thought Moses. *The bush should be all burned up and the flames gone.* But still the bush burned.
Move Moses closer to the bush.	So Moses walked over to the bush, curious as to why the bush did not burn up. As Moses came up close to the bush, a voice from within the bush called, "Moses! Moses!" Moses replied, "Here I am!"
Point to the bush.	God said, "Take off your sandals, for you are standing on holy ground." God continued, "I am the God of Abraham, Isaac, and Jacob."
Cover your face with your hands.	Moses hid his face because he was afraid.
Point to the bush.	Then God said, "My people in Egypt are suffering. I am going to deliver them out of Egypt and bring them to a good land, the land I promised to give to Abraham. Go to Pharaoh and tell him to let my people go."
Point to Moses.	Moses said, "What if they don't believe me or listen to me?"
Point to the bush.	God said, "What is in your hand?"
Present the staff.	Moses replied, "A staff." God said, "Throw it on the ground."
Put the staff on the underlay.	Moses threw his staff on the ground and it became a snake. God said, "Reach out your hand and take it by the tail." Moses did so.

Pick up the staff.   The snake turned back into a shepherd's staff. "This," said God, "is so Pharaoh and the people will believe that I, the God of Abraham, Isaac, and Jacob, have appeared to you. If they do not believe this sign, then take some water from the Nile River and pour it on the dry ground. It will become blood on the ground. Now go! I will be with you."

Move Moses and the sheep near Jethro.   So Moses went back to Jethro and said, "I must go back to my own people in Egypt."

Pause and reflect on the whole scene.

Begin the wondering time.

I wonder what it was like for Moses to live in the palace.

I wonder what it was like to be one of God's people and work so hard for the Pharaoh.

I wonder why Moses went out to see how his people were doing.

I wonder how Moses felt when he ran away to Midian.

I wonder how Moses felt about caring for sheep in the desert every day.

I wonder how different it was to live in the desert instead of the palace.

I wonder how Moses felt when God talked to him from the bush.

I wonder how Moses felt about going back to Egypt.

I wonder if the people will accept him as leader.

I wonder if they will listen to him.

I wonder what will happen when Moses goes before Pharaoh and says, "God says, 'Let my people go.'"

Return to the worship outline and continue.

11

The Ten Plagues

Scripture sources: Exodus 4:29–12:42; Joshua 24:5; Hebrews 11:27–28

Materials:

Figures of Moses and Pharaoh

Green underlay (44" x 36")

Shepherd's staff

10 4" x 6" cards, numbered on the back and covered with clear Con-Tact paper, illustrating the plagues:

1. red
2. picture of frogs
3. picture of gnats
4. picture of flies
5. picture of animals
6. picture of people and animals
7. picture of hail, rain, lightning
8. picture of locusts
9. black
10. with words "first born"

Basket to hold materials

Scripture to read: Exodus 5:1–2; 10:21–29; 12:7–8, 12–13, 31

Bible marker: A picture of Moses telling the Pharaoh, "God says, 'Let my people go!'"

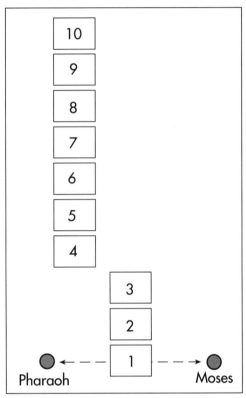

Leader

Carefully spread out the green underlay the long way with the 36" side near the leader. Present Moses and hold him as you say:

Moses, who was now eighty years old, obeyed God. He started the long trip back to Egypt.

Set Moses down on the right side of the underlay.

When he arrived in Egypt, he called all the leaders of God's people together and told them what God had said.

Hold up the staff. Place it on the underlay near Moses.

He showed them what happened to his staff when he threw it down and what happened to the water from the Nile River when he poured it on the ground.

Make a circular motion with your hand around Moses indicating a large group of people.

God's people were so happy that they bowed down and worshiped. God was going to help them. God was going to deliver them from the cruel Egyptians.

Present Pharaoh and set him on the left side of the underlay. Move Moses next to Pharaoh.

Moses went to Pharaoh and said, "The Lord, the God of Israel, says, 'Let my people go so they can worship me.'"

Point to Pharaoh.

But Pharaoh said, "Who is the Lord that I should listen to him? Why should I obey the Lord? I don't know the Lord and I will *not* let the people go."

Move Moses back to the right side.

Point to Pharaoh.

Then Pharaoh said to his slave drivers and foremen, "Do not give the people any more straw to make bricks. They must find their own straw but still make just as many bricks as before. The people are lazy and have too much time. That is why they are thinking up things like asking to worship their God."

With a sweeping motion of your hand, indicate a large group of people around Moses.

The people complained to Moses. "Now look what has happened since you asked Pharaoh to let us go. We get no straw and still have to make the same number of bricks as before."

Point to Moses.

Moses said to God, "Oh, Lord, look at all this trouble. Instead of letting us go, Pharaoh has only made the work harder."

God replied, "I will deliver my people. Because of my mighty hand, Pharaoh will let my people go. I am the Lord. I will bring my people to the land I promised to Abraham."

God continued, "Go to Pharaoh again. Show him the staff that turns into a snake. Show him the water becoming blood. Tell him 'God says, Let my people go.'"

Move Moses back to Pharaoh.

So once more Moses went to Pharaoh with God's words.

Hold up the staff. Place it on the underlay near Moses.

He threw his staff on the ground and it became a snake. Pharaoh's wise men did the same thing, but Moses' snake swallowed up their snakes. Moses said to Pharaoh, "God says, 'Let my people go so they can worship me!'"

Point to Pharaoh.

Pharaoh's heart was hard and he said, "No!"

Point to Moses.

God said to Moses, "I will show Pharaoh that I am the Lord. I will send wonders and signs to Pharaoh and his people so they will know that I am the Lord. In the morning stretch your staff over the Nile River and the river will turn to blood!"

Pick up the staff.

In the morning Moses stretched his staff over the Nile River and it turned to blood.

Lay the staff down by Moses. Hold up the red card.

All the fish died and the river smelled awful. No one could drink from the river.

Place the red card on the top middle of the underlay.

Point to Pharaoh.

Still Pharaoh said, "No!"

Hold up the card of frogs.

Next God sent frogs that covered everything. Frogs were in the houses, in the beds, in the ovens, and on the tables. Frogs were in the fields and the yards. Frogs were everywhere!

Lay the frog card below the red card.

Point to Pharaoh.

Still Pharaoh said, "No!"

Hold up the card of gnats.

This time God turned the dust into gnats. Gnats covered the people and the animals. All the dust in the whole land turned to gnats.

Lay the gnat card below the frog card.

Point to Pharaoh.

Still Pharaoh said, "No!"

Point to Moses.

God told Moses to tell Pharaoh, "The Lord says, 'Let my people go so they may worship me. If you will not let my people go, I will send swarms of flies on you and your people. Your houses will be full of flies. But where my people live there will be no flies so that you will know that I am the Lord.'" So Moses told Pharaoh God's words.

Hold up the card of flies.

And the flies came in swarms. They filled the palace and the houses. Flies were everywhere in Egypt but not where God's people lived. From now on no terrible thing would happen to God's people. The plagues would come only to Pharaoh and his people.

Place the card of flies on the underlay on the far left to indicate that the flies were only in Egypt.

Still Pharaoh said, "No!"

Hold up the card of animals.

Next God sent a terrible disease on all the Egyptian livestock: the horses, the donkeys, the camels, the cattle, the sheep, and the goats. All the animals that were left outside died from the disease.

Lay the animal card below the card of flies.

Still Pharaoh said, "No!"

Hold up the card of people and animals.

Next God sent terrible sores on the people and on the animals that were still alive.

Lay the card below the previous card.

Still Pharaoh said, "No!"

Hold up the card of hail.

Next God sent a hailstorm, the worst hailstorm that had ever fallen on Egypt. Any people or animals that were outside died because of the hailstorm. It also ruined the crops.

Lay the card of hail below the previous one.

Still Pharaoh said, "No!"

Hold up the card of locusts.

Next, God sent locusts. Any plants that the hail had not destroyed, the locusts ate. They ate the crops. They ate the trees. They filled every house. They were so thick on the ground, that the ground looked black. Nothing green remained.

Lay the card below the previous one.

Still Pharaoh said, "No!"

Hold up the black card.

For the ninth time God sent an awful plague on Pharaoh and his country. This time there was total darkness in all of Egypt. The people could not see anyone or anything. For three days no one went anywhere.

But where God's people lived there was light!

Lay the black card below the previous one.

Still Pharaoh said, "No!" He said to Moses, "Get out of my sight. I do not want to see you again!"

Move Moses back to the right side.

So Moses left Pharaoh and never saw him again.

Again God spoke to Moses, "Tell the people to get ready. They are to kill a year-old lamb, take some of the blood, and put it on the doorframes of their homes. They are to roast the lamb and eat it with unleavened bread or bread made without yeast. They must eat with their coats and shoes on and their staffs in their hands because it is the Lord's Passover."

God's people did as Moses told them. They killed a year-old lamb and put its blood on the sides and tops of the doorframes of their homes. They roasted the lamb and ate it with unleavened bread.

Hold up the tenth card. Lay it below the previous one.

Now God sent the tenth plague. The firstborn of all the Egyptian families and animals died. But not the people of God.

Cup your hand over Moses and pass your other hand over him.

They were safe because the blood was on their doorframes. Death "passed over" them. Pharaoh sent word to Moses. "Up! Leave! Go, worship the Lord. Take everyone and all your flocks and herds. Go!"

Pause and reflect on the whole scene.

Begin the wondering time.

I wonder what it was like to live in Egypt when all the plagues came.

I wonder why Pharaoh was so stubborn.

I wonder what the people in Pharaoh's land thought when all these horrible things came.

I wonder how God's people felt when the horrible things happened and they were spared.

I wonder what the people were thinking as they prepared the lamb.

I wonder how God's people felt when they heard Pharaoh's word, "Go!"

Return to the worship outline and continue.

12

Manna and Water

Scripture source: Exodus 15:22–17:7

Materials:

    Figures of Moses, ten adults, and children

    Sand-colored underlay

    3" circle of blue felt for water

    2" square of sheer, white material for manna

    1/4" dowel cut into one 5" piece and one 3" piece

    Rock

    Basket to hold the figures

    Tray to hold all materials

Scripture to read: Exodus 16:13–16; 17:1, 5–6

Bible marker: A picture of people picking up manna to eat to help us remember how God gave his people water and food in the desert

Children

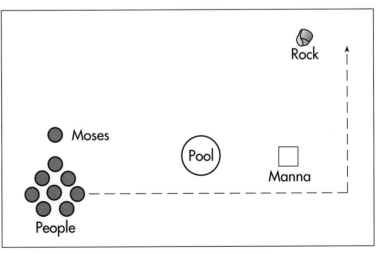

Leader

Carefully spread out the sand-colored underlay.

God's people were now free from the Pharaoh's rule.

Place Moses and the people one by one on the left corner.

God had sent the Ten Plagues, which were so bad that Pharaoh finally told the people to leave. They had come safely through the Red Sea and were now in the desert. They moved from place to place in the desert.

Move people to the middle near edge.

They came to a place called Marah. They had taken all the food that they could carry with them but they needed water to drink. At Marah there was a pool of water,

Place the pool of blue felt near the people.

but the water was very bitter and the people could not drink it. The people asked Moses what they were supposed to drink because they were thirsty.

Present the smaller piece of wood.

God showed Moses a piece of wood. When Moses threw the wood into the water, the water became sweet and the people could drink it.

Put it on the blue felt.

God said, "Obey me. I am the Lord, the one who cares and provides for you."

Move people to the near left corner.

The people left that place and wandered into an area of the desert called Zin.

They had been away from Egypt for some time. Their food supply was running out, and the people were getting hungry. They began to wish they had stayed in Egypt where there was plenty of food.

God heard the people complaining and told Moses that he would cause food to fall from the sky. Every morning the people were to go into the desert and collect enough food for that day.

Present the sheer cloth.

The next morning there was something thin and flaky on the ground in the desert.

Lay the cloth down on the underlay.

When the people saw it they called it "manna," which means, "what is it?"

Point to Moses.

Moses told the people that this was the bread that God was giving them. Each day they collected the manna in the morning.

Move the people to the far right corner of the underlay.

Now the people came to a place where there was nothing to drink. Again the people cried out to Moses. They wanted something to drink.

Arrange the people into a circle.

They said, "Why did you bring us out of Egypt? Did you want us to die of thirst?" Moses prayed to God and asked what he should do. God answered Moses, "Take some of the leaders of the people with you and go ahead of the people. Take your long stick and strike the rock that I will show you and water will come out of it for the people."

Move Moses and a few people away from the group.

So Moses took some of the leaders and moved ahead of the people.

Place the rock near them.

They found the rock that God had spoken about.

Strike the rock with the larger stick and unroll the blue felt.

Moses took his walking stick and hit the rock. Water began to come out of the rock for all the people to drink.

Move the rest of the people around the rock in a circle.

God took care of his people by giving them bread to eat and water to drink.

Pause and reflect on the whole scene.

Begin the wondering time.

I wonder what it would be like to have neither food to eat nor water to drink.

I wonder what it was like to go out every morning and pick up manna.

I wonder what the manna tasted like.

I wonder if the people were thankful that God gave them food and water.

I wonder how God takes care of us.

Return to the worship outline and continue.

13

Moses' Helpers

Scripture source: Exodus 18
Materials:
   Figures, underlay, and tray from the previous story
Scripture to read: Exodus 18:24–26
Bible marker: A picture of Moses to remind us of the
   time when God helped Moses choose helpers to rule
   God's people

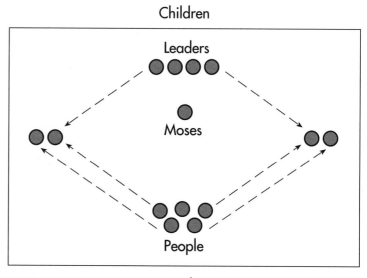

Carefully spread out the sand-colored underlay. Place some of the people on the underlay.

The people of God journeyed through the desert.

Present Moses.

Moses, the one who had led them out of Pharaoh's trap and through the water to freedom, was their chosen leader. Because he was their leader, the people came to him with all their grumblings.

Bring four people forward to Moses.

But Moses was tired and weary of listening to their grumblings. They grumbled about no food to eat and they grumbled about no water to drink. They grumbled about being out in the desert all of the time. Some of them even wanted to go back to Egypt. The air no longer rang with sounds of

Spread hands in an arc in the air.

rejoicing.

Spread hands in straight line horizontally.

The laughter was gone.

Extend hands out to the side as if to reach for another and then close hands in fists.

The people no longer joined hands, dancing and singing praises to God as they had done when they came through the waters to freedom.

Place two figures opposite one another.

Sometimes the people argued between themselves. Even friends said ugly words and shouted at each other.

Place two more figures opposite one another.

Mothers and fathers quarreled.

Put one or more children opposite two other figures.

Children did not obey their parents.

God heard his quarrelsome people and was sad. He wanted to heal their hearts so they could be happy again. So God helped Moses choose certain people from out of all the people of Israel to be his helpers.

Have several figures come forward to Moses.

Moses taught these people about loving God and loving people. Then Moses set them over the people to settle their disagreements.

Place the figures in front of the various groupings of figures.

These people were called the judges or helpers. They helped the people understand how to love God and how to love each other so all the people could live in peace.

Bring figures together as if touching and holding hands in harmony.

Pause and reflect on the whole scene.

Begin the wondering time.

I wonder how the people felt when they were grumbling and complaining and arguing.

I wonder how it felt to have people who loved God and loved people to help settle the arguing and the quarreling.

I wonder if the hearts of the people were filled with joy.

I wonder how Moses felt after he had helpers to help him lead God's people.

I wonder if you have ever argued or grumbled and if someone brought you peace.

I wonder if you can help bring peace between other children who may be arguing and grumbling.

I wonder what will happen to God's people next.

Return to the worship outline and continue.

14

The Twelve Spies

Scripture sources: Numbers 9:15–23, 13–14; Deuteronomy 1:19–2:1

Materials:

    Figures of Moses and twelve men

    Sand-colored underlay

    Piece of wood with a picture of a cloud on one side, fire on the other

    A picture of grapes

    Basket for the figures

    Tray to hold all materials

Scripture to read: Numbers 13:1–2, 21a, 26–28a, 30–31; 14:26–34

Bible marker: A picture of a large cluster of grapes to remind us of the spies and how ten brought back a bad report and two said God would help them enter the Promised Land

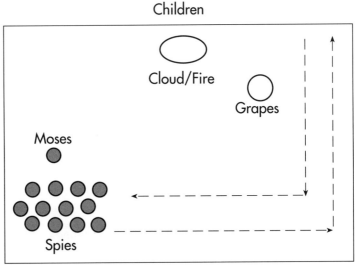

Children

Cloud/Fire

Grapes

Moses

Spies

Leader

Carefully spread out the underlay. Place the people on the near left corner of the underlay.

The people of God had been in the desert for a long time. God had brought them out of Egypt. Every day God had given them bread to eat and water to drink. Sometimes God even gave them meat to eat. God had given them the Ten Best Ways to Live and had told them how to build the ark, a special place to keep the Ten Best Ways to Live. (These are also called the Ten Commandments.) God had told them how to build the tabernacle, a special place to worship God, and how to take it with them when they moved.

Present the cloud.

During the day a special cloud covered the tabernacle.

Turn the cloud to the fire side.

During the night the cloud looked like fire. When the cloud moved, God's people moved. When the cloud rested, God's people rested.

Set the cloud/fire on the underlay.

Now the people of God were very close to the land that God had promised to give them.

Point to Moses.

God said to Moses, "Choose some men to explore the Promised Land. Choose one man from each of the twelve tribes of my people." Moses chose twelve men.

Move the twelve figures slightly away from Moses.

Moses told these men, "Go up into the Promised Land. See what the land is like. Are the cities big or small? Are there trees in the land or not? Try to bring back some of the fruit."

Continue moving the twelve figures toward the near right corner as you say:

Now the spies did as Moses had told them. They began at the south end of the Promised Land and walked way up to the north end. They checked out the people and the land, the towns and the cities. They checked out the crops, the food, and the trees. They did just as Moses had told them to.

Move the figures to the far right corner. Turn them around and begin moving them back.

When the men had gotten to the north end of the Promised Land, they turned around. Slowly the men walked through the land. The men remembered that Moses had asked them to bring back some fruit. Along with some other fruit, the men took a branch bearing a single cluster of grapes back to Moses.

Present the grape picture. Lay it on the underlay.

The cluster of grapes was so large that it had to be carried on a pole by two men.

Have the twelve spies rejoin Moses.	Now all the spies were back, and the people gathered to hear what they had to say. Was the land good or bad? Were the people strong or weak? Were there many people or few people? What kinds of towns did the people live in? How was the soil? Were there trees in the land? The people and Moses had so many questions. They listened eagerly to the report of the twelve spies.
Point to the spies.	The spies said, "The land is very, very good. Look at this fruit! But the people who live there are very big and powerful and their cities are large and strong."
Set apart two of the spies.	Then Caleb and Joshua, two of the spies, said, "We can live in the land. God is with us."
Point to the ten spies.	"No!" said the ten spies. "We can't take the land. The people are giants. They are so big we seemed like grasshoppers!" The ten spies were afraid and gave a bad report.
Point to Caleb and Joshua.	Only Caleb and Joshua gave a good report. "We can go into the land. It is a good land, and God will be with us! Don't be afraid."
	The rest of the people wanted to stone Caleb and Joshua.
Hold up the cloud.	Then God spoke to Moses from the cloud and said, "I am angry with these people. Don't they remember all I did for them? I brought them out of Egypt. I gave them food and water. I showed them the way through the desert. I gave them the Ten Best Ways to Live. Now why are the people afraid? I am with them!"
Set the cloud back down.	
Point to Moses.	Moses said, "Oh, God, please forgive your people."
Pause.	God said, "I forgive the people for not trusting me, but not one of them will enter the Promised Land. Not one of the people who saw all the wonders I did in Egypt and in the desert, not one of the grown-up people who left Egypt will enter the Promised Land. No one who is twenty years old and older will see the Promised Land."
Point to Caleb and Joshua.	God continued, "Only Caleb and Joshua who trusted me and gave a good report will enter the Promised Land."

Point to the rest of the people.

"Now turn around and go back to the desert. For forty days the spies explored the Promised Land. Now for forty years, one year for each day, you will live in the desert and remember that you did not trust me."

Turn each figure around.

And so God's people had to stay in the desert for forty more years because they grumbled and complained and listened to the bad report of the ten spies instead of the good report of Caleb and Joshua.

Pause and reflect on the whole scene.

Begin the wondering time.

I wonder what is was like to live in the desert.

I wonder how the people felt when they got close to the Promised Land.

I wonder how the twelve felt when Moses chose them to be spies.

I wonder what they were thinking as they walked through the Promised Land.

I wonder if it was hard for the people to wait for forty days while the spies were gone.

I wonder why ten spies gave a bad report and only two spies gave a good report.

I wonder why the people believed the ten and not the two.

I wonder how the people felt when God told them they had to spend forty more years in the desert.

I wonder if the people learned anything.

I wonder what will happen to God's people now.

I wonder if they will ever enter the Promised Land.

Return to the worship outline and continue.

15

Jonah

Scripture source: Jonah

Materials:

    Figure of a large fish with shape of Jonah cut out of the middle

    Green underlay

    Blue material (18" x 22") to cover half of green underlay

    City of Nineveh background

    Boat-shaped basket

    Tray to hold materials

Scripture to read: Jonah 1:1–6, 15–17; 2:10; 3:1–3; (chapter 4 with the older children)

Bible marker: A picture of Jonah preaching to the people of Nineveh to help us remember that God loved Jonah and God loved the people

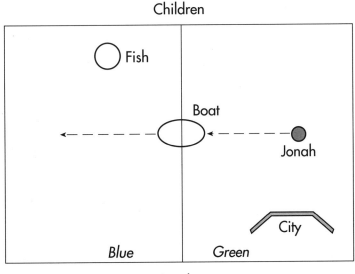

83

Carefully spread out the green underlay. Present Jonah.

Jonah lived a long time ago.

One day God came to Jonah and said, "Go to the city of Nineveh. The people need to hear about me. They are mean and cruel and need to change their ways. They need to love God and love people."

Shake head "no!"

Jonah did not want to go to Nineveh. He knew about the people of Nineveh and how badly they behaved.

Set Jonah down on the right side of the underlay. Carefully spread out the blue material, covering the left half of the green.

Instead of obeying God, Jonah decided to run away.

Add the boat basket to the scene. Place it in the middle of the underlay, half on the green, half on the blue.

Jonah went to the seacoast, bought a ticket, and climbed on board a boat that was sailing in the opposite direction from Nineveh.

Place Jonah in the boat basket and move it onto the blue part of the underlay.

But God was watching Jonah. He knew what Jonah was doing. God sent a great wind to blow the sea into huge, rocking waves.

Pick up the boat basket and rock it back and forth.

The sailors were afraid the boat would sink so they threw the cargo into the sea. Everyone was afraid except for Jonah, who had gone to the bottom of the boat to sleep.

Continue holding the boat, rocking it back and forth as though tossed about by the waves.

"Wake up!" said the ship's captain. "How can you sleep in such a storm?"

Point to Jonah.

Jonah knew God had sent the storm. He told the captain and sailors to throw him into the water so the storm would stop.

With one hand holding the boat, use the other hand to pick up Jonah.

So the men threw Jonah into the water.

Put Jonah into the water.

Immediately the storm stopped and the sea became calm.

Set the boat down on the water (blue underlay). Present the large fish and place Jonah in the middle of it while you say:

God sent a great big fish to swallow Jonah. For three days and nights Jonah was inside the big fish.

Pause.

Jonah prayed while he was inside the big fish. God told the big fish to spit Jonah up on the beach. The big fish did what God wanted.

Take Jonah figure out of the fish. Set the fish on the blue half of the underlay. Place Jonah on the green half of the underlay.

Again God came to Jonah and said, "Go to the great city of Nineveh and tell them about me."

This time Jonah listened.

Place the city background on the right side of the underlay.

Jonah went to Nineveh.

Place Jonah in front of the background.

As soon as he entered the gates, he began telling the people, "In forty days, God will destroy your city. Change your ways. Love God and love people."

With a sweeping hand motion, indicate a large group of people.

The people were sorry for the bad things they had done and said. Even the king was sorry. They all took off their good, clothes and wore sackcloth—rough clothes made of camels' hair. They asked God to forgive them for the bad things they had done.

God was very happy. The people had changed and now God would not destroy the city.

Add this ending for older children: Point to Jonah.

But Jonah was unhappy. He wanted God to destroy Nineveh.

Move Jonah to the far edge of the green underlay.

So Jonah went outside the city walls and sat down to watch what would happen. It was hot and Jonah built a little shelter to shade him from the sun. God caused a vine to grow and shade Jonah even more.

The next morning God sent a worm to eat the vine.

Point to Jonah.   This made Jonah angry.

God said, "You feel sorry for the plant and for yourself! But you do not feel sorry for all the people of Nineveh!

Shouldn't I forgive all the people who turn to me and are sorry for the bad things they do?"

Pause and reflect on the whole scene.

Begin the wondering time.

I wonder how Jonah felt when he disobeyed God and ran away.

I wonder how everyone on the boat felt when the big storm came.

I wonder what it was like to throw Jonah overboard.

I wonder what Jonah thought would happen to him when the sailors threw him overboard.

I wonder what it was like to be in the stomach of a big fish for three days and three nights.

I wonder how Jonah felt when all the people in Nineveh were sorry for the bad things they did.

Add these thoughts for older children:

I wonder why Jonah wanted God to destroy Nineveh.

I wonder why God used a vine and a worm to teach Jonah a lesson.

I wonder if now Jonah will listen better to what God tells him to do.

Return to the worship outline and continue.

New Testament Stories from the Gospels

Mary Visits Elizabeth

Scripture sources: Luke 1:26–56; 1 Samuel 2:1–10; Isaiah 7:14; 9:6–7; Jeremiah 23:5–6

Materials:

Figures of Mary, Elizabeth, and angel

Purple underlay

Beige felt road (6" x 36")

Background with Mary's house on one side and Elizabeth's house on the other side

Basket to hold figures

Scripture to read: Luke 1:26–32a, 38–40, 46–49

Bible marker: A picture of Elizabeth and Mary to remind us of the special babies God was sending to both mothers

Children

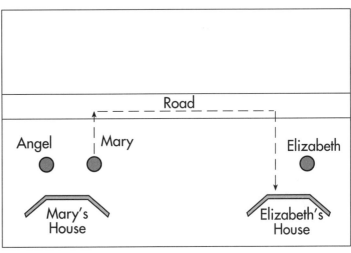

Leader

89

Carefully spread out the purple underlay.	We are in the season of Advent. It is time to get ready to celebrate Jesus' birthday on Christmas.
Place Mary's house on the left of the underlay.	It all begins in Nazareth, a small town in Galilee.
Present Mary.	Mary was a young girl who was engaged to be married to a carpenter named Joseph.
Place Mary in front of the house.	Mary was excitedly getting ready for her wedding. She and Joseph were poor and could not afford a big wedding. But their wedding would be special because Mary and Joseph loved each other very much. They also loved God and would have a home filled with God's love.
Present the angel.	One day as Mary was busily working at home, she was startled by an angel, Gabriel, standing right in the room where she was.
Put the angel next to Mary.	The angel said, "Greetings. You are favored by God. The Lord is with you."
Point to Mary.	Mary was startled and frightened. What did the angel mean when he said, "You are favored by God?"
Point to the angel.	The angel spoke again, "Do not be afraid, Mary. You have found favor with God. God has a special plan for you. You have been chosen to be the mother of a son whose name shall be Jesus, which means salvation, because he will save his people from their sins. He will be great, the Son of God. He will be a king forever."
Point to Mary.	But Mary did not understand. "How can this be?" she wondered. "How can I have a baby? Joseph and I are not yet married."
Point to the angel.	The angel answered, "The Holy Spirit will come to you, and God's power will be on you. This baby is God's son. God will be his Father." Then the angel told Mary about her relative, Elizabeth, who would soon have a baby. "Six months ago Elizabeth found that she would have a baby even though she is old." The angel continued, "Every promise God makes comes true."

Point to Mary. When Mary heard all this, she said, "I am God's servant. I will do whatever the Lord wants. Let everything happen as you said." Then the angel was gone.

Return the angel figure to the basket. Mary hurriedly packed the things she needed. She was going to visit Elizabeth.

Add the felt road from the left side to the right side across the middle of the underlay.

Place Mary on the road. Turn the house to the other side and set it on the right side of the underlay. She began her trip.

Zechariah and Elizabeth's home was in the hill country of Judea. It was a long way for Mary to walk from Nazareth to Judea but Mary wanted to see Elizabeth. She wanted to tell Elizabeth that she, Mary, would be the mother of God's son.

Slowly move Mary along the road. Oh, so many thoughts went through Mary's mind as she walked over the dusty roads. Finally she arrived at Zechariah and Elizabeth's home.

Present Elizabeth and add her to the house scene. Elizabeth was overjoyed to see Mary. What a special treat to have Mary come for a visit!

Place Mary next to Elizabeth. When Elizabeth saw Mary, she was filled with the Spirit of God and said, "Blessed are you among women, and blessed is the child you will have! Why is it that the mother of my Lord should come to visit me? Blessed are you because you believe that what the Lord says will come true!"

Point to Mary. Then Mary, filled with the Holy Spirit, sang a song of praise. "My soul glorifies the Lord and my spirit rejoices in God, my Savior. God has taken notice of me, his humble servant."

Point to Elizabeth. Mary stayed with Elizabeth for about three months and then returned home to Nazareth.

Pause and reflect on the whole scene.

Begin the wondering time.

I wonder how Mary felt when the angel appeared to her.

I wonder about the angel's words to Mary, "Greetings, you are favored by God."

I wonder what Mary was thinking as she traveled to Elizabeth's home.

I wonder what Mary and Elizabeth talked about for the three months Mary stayed with Elizabeth.

I wonder why God chose Mary to be the mother of Jesus.

Return to the worship outline and continue.

17

Christmas

Scripture sources: Luke 2:1–20; Matthew 1:18–25
Materials:
  Figures of Mary, Joseph, baby, shepherds, sheep, and
    angel (optional: donkeys)
  White underlay (or purple if you tell this story dur-
    ing the season of Advent)
  Beige felt road (6" x 36")
  Stable with a manger filled with hay or straw
  Basket to hold figures
  Tray to hold materials
Scripture to read: Luke 2:1–20
Bible marker: A picture of Mary, Joseph, and baby
  Jesus to remind us of the special gift God sent at
  Christmas to show us how much God loves us

Children

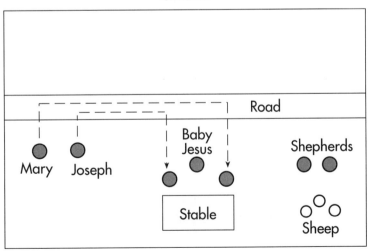

Leader

Carefully spread out the white (or purple) underlay. Present Mary and Joseph. Set them on the left edge of the underlay.

Not long after Mary returned to Nazareth from her visit to Elizabeth, the Roman ruler, Caesar Augustus, decided he needed to know the number of people who lived in the countries he ruled. He commanded the people to travel to the cities and towns from which their families came. There they would have their names written down on a list.

Point to Mary and Joseph.

Both Mary and Joseph came from the family of King David, so they needed to travel to Bethlehem, the place where King David had lived as a boy.

Add the felt road across the middle of the underlay from left to right. Slowly move Mary and Joseph along the road.

It was a long trip from Nazareth to Bethlehem, down the mountains to the Jordan River. They followed the Jordan River almost to its end and then went up the mountains to Bethlehem.

Stop Mary and Joseph in the middle of the road.

By the time Mary and Joseph came to Bethlehem, it was full of people who had come, like them, to be counted for Caesar Augustus. Mary and Joseph needed to find a place to sleep because Mary's baby was coming soon. They looked and looked, but each place was already filled with other travelers.

Finally a kindly innkeeper offered them the stable behind the inn where the animals ate and slept.

Add the stable behind Mary and Joseph.

It wasn't fancy but it was quiet, dry, and a place where Mary and Joseph could be alone.

Add the animals and manger to the stable scene.

That night, in the stable, Jesus was born.

Present Jesus and place him in the manger.

Mary carefully took her new baby and wrapped him in cloths and laid him in the manger, the place where the animals ate their hay.

Pause. Indicate the near right corner of the underlay with a sweeping motion of your hand.

Outside of Bethlehem there were some grassy fields.

Present and add the shepherds and sheep on the near right side.

Here shepherds were taking care of their sheep. It was nighttime and everything was quiet.

Present the angel. Hold him until you put him back in the basket.

Suddenly an angel appeared, and a bright light shone all around them.

Point to the shepherds.	The shepherds were frightened. The angel said kindly, "Do not be afraid. I have good news. It is the most wonderful news for you and everyone else. Today in Bethlehem, a Savior, God's Son, has been born. He is Christ, the Lord. You can go to see him. You will know he is the Savior by this sign: He is a newborn baby wrapped in cloths and lying in a manger."
Using your free hand, with a sweeping motion, indicate the whole area around the angel and above the shepherds.	And then the air around the shepherds and the whole sky was filled with angels, a great choir of angels singing and praising God, saying, "Glory to God! Glory to God in the Highest and on earth peace, goodwill to men."
Pause. Place the angel back in the basket.	As the shepherds looked in wonder and listened, the angels disappeared from sight.
Point to the shepherds.	The shepherds said to each other, "Let's go to Bethlehem at once and see this wonderful thing that the Lord has told us about."
Move the shepherds and sheep to the stable.	As quickly as they could, the shepherds hurried to Bethlehem. There they found Joseph, Mary, and baby Jesus. Just as the angel had told them, the baby was wrapped in cloths and lying in a manger.
Point to the shepherds.	The shepherds told Mary and Joseph about the angel and what he had said and about the angel choir and their song.
Point to Mary.	Mary listened carefully and kept the words in her heart.
Point to the shepherds.	The shepherds were so happy that they told the news to everyone they saw: "Jesus is born! God sent his son! The Savior has come! We saw him ourselves. How much God loves us!"

Pause and reflect on the whole scene.

Begin the wondering time.

I wonder what Mary and Joseph thought when they heard the news that they needed to go to Bethlehem.

I wonder what it was like for Mary and Joseph to travel that long way to Bethlehem.

I wonder how they felt when they arrived in Bethlehem and every inn was full.

I wonder what it was like to stay in a stable.

I wonder how Mary and Joseph felt when Jesus was born.

I wonder how the shepherds felt when they saw the angel.

I wonder how the shepherds felt when the sky was full of angels.

I wonder how we can be like the shepherds and tell the good news of Jesus.

I wonder whom we can tell about the coming of Jesus.

Return to the worship outline and continue.

18

Jesus' First Miracle

Scripture source: John 2:1–11

Materials:

> Figures of Jesus, Mary, three disciples, two servants, and wedding host
> Green underlay
> Six jars and a small basin
> Small table
> Plates and cups (optional)
> House background
> Baskets to hold figures, jars, basin, plates, and cups
> Tray to hold materials

Scripture to read: John 2:1–3, 6–11

Bible marker: A picture of Jesus turning water into wine to help us remember that Jesus came to earth to do God's work

Children

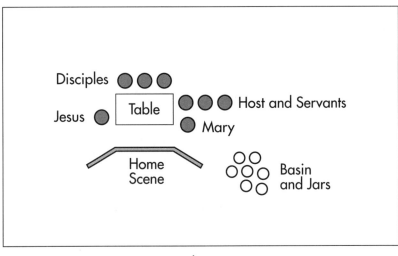

Leader

Carefully spread out the green underlay. Present Jesus.

Jesus grew from a baby to a boy to a young man. It was time for him to begin the work God had sent him into the world to do.

Place Jesus on the middle of the underlay. Present each disciple and set him next to Jesus.

Jesus had called his disciples to follow him and learn from him so they could tell others about God.

Place the home background behind the figures.

Jesus and his disciples had been invited to a wedding in the nearby village of Cana. Weddings were happy, important times. Friends and family gathered for a great feast, which could last a whole week. Every day the guests would talk, laugh, eat, and celebrate the wedding of the bride and groom. It was a happy time!

Present the jars and set them to the right of the home scene.

Because the roads were dusty in Jesus' time, and people wore sandals on their feet, it was the custom to have large jars of water in a home for washing feet and hands.

Present the small basin and set it near the jars. With a cupping motion of the hand put "water" from the jar into the basin. Then with hand motions show the washing of feet.

Family members and guests could take some of the water from the jar, put it into a smaller basin, and wash their dusty, dirty feet as they entered the home.

With hand motions show the washing of hands.

It was also the custom to wash their hands before every meal.

Add the table to the home scene. Move Jesus and his disciples around the table.

After washing their feet and hands, the family and friends would gather for the feast.

Place the cups and plates on the table.

There was plenty of food to eat. Fruits, vegetables, meat, and breads covered the table. People drank wine with their meals, so there was plenty of wine to drink.

Present the host and servants and add them to the scene.

The wedding host directed the servants to keep the tables full of food and the cups full of wine.

Present Mary and set her in the home scene.	Mary, Jesus' mother, was also a guest at the wedding. She enjoyed this time with her son and his friends. There was talk and laughter. Everyone joined in the conversation and good wishes.
Move the servants off to the side.	As Mary talked and ate, she noticed the servants off to the side talking among themselves. They had worried looks on their faces. Mary wondered what was wrong.
Move Mary over to the servants.	Mary walked over to the servants. "What is wrong?" she asked quietly.
Point to the servants.	"We're all out of wine," the servants told her. "We don't know what to do. The wedding feast is far from over and there is no more wine to drink. What should we do?"
Point to Mary.	"Wait here," Mary told them.
Move Mary next to Jesus.	Quickly Mary went back to Jesus. She whispered, "The wine is all gone."
Point to Jesus.	Jesus turned to Mary and said, "But it's not my wedding. I'm not the host here."
Move Mary back to the servants.	Mary returned to the servants. "Do whatever Jesus tells you," she told them.
Move Jesus from the table to where the servants are.	Jesus walked over to the servants.
Point to the jars.	He looked at the big water jars that were now empty because everyone had washed their feet and hands. He said to the servants, "Fill the jars with water."
Point to the servants. With a cupping motion of the hand "fill" the jars.	The servants quickly went to work. They filled all six jars with clear, cold water from the well. When the jars were full, Jesus said, "Now take some out and take it to the wedding host." The servants did as they were told. As they took some of the water out of a jar, they looked at each other in surprise. This wasn't water anymore! It was wine! Jesus had turned the water into wine!
Move the servants next to the wedding host.	They quickly took it to the wedding host, who tasted it. This was not only wine but good wine! It was even better than the first wine that was served to the guests.

Point to the disciples. The disciples were impressed. Jesus really was powerful. Jesus really was God's Son. They believed in Jesus.

Pause and reflect on the whole scene.

Begin the wondering time.

I wonder what it was like to go to a wedding with Jesus.

I wonder how the servants felt when the wine was gone.

I wonder why Mary told Jesus about the wine.

I wonder how the wedding host felt when he tasted the water Jesus turned into wine.

The servants obeyed Jesus and filled the jars with water. Who do we need to obey and why?

What happened when the servants obeyed?

I wonder how the disciples felt when they saw Jesus' power.

Return to the worship outline and continue.

19

Jesus Heals Peter's Mother-in-Law

Scripture sources: Matthew 8:14–17; Mark 1:29–35; Luke 4:38–41

Materials:

   Figures of Jesus, Peter, mother-in-law, two disciples, and a man

   Green underlay

   Mat

   Background with the inside of house on one side and synagogue on the other side

   Basket to hold figures

Scripture to read: Mark 1:30–34a

Bible marker: A picture of Jesus healing people to remind us of Jesus' great power—so great he could heal Peter's mother-in-law of her fever and all others of their sickness

Children

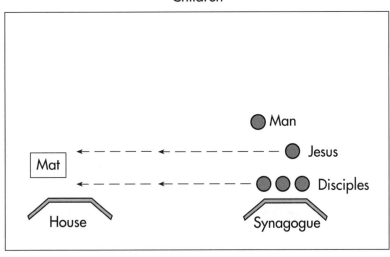

Leader

Carefully spread out the green underlay. Place the synagogue on the right side of the underlay.

This is a synagogue, a place to worship God. Each Sabbath day, Jesus and his disciples would go to the synagogue to worship.

Present Jesus and the disciples and place them in the synagogue.

In the synagogue, Jesus and his disciples could pray, listen to God's words, and praise God. It was a happy, joyous time to be in God's house with many others who also worshiped.

Point to Jesus.

Sometimes Jesus would teach. He told the people to love God and to love each other. He told them stories about the Kingdom of God. The people were impressed. Jesus was a much better teacher than the teachers they usually listened to.

Present the man and set him in the synagogue scene.

All of a sudden, a man with evil spirits living in him called out, "Why are you bothering us, Jesus of Nazareth? I know you are the Holy Son of God."

Point to Jesus.

Jesus said sternly, "Be quiet!" He commanded the evil spirits to come out of the man. The evil spirits obeyed and the man was healed. The evil spirits no longer lived in him, making him do and say strange things. Jesus had made him all better.

Indicate with a sweeping motion of the hand all the others in the synagogue.

All the people were amazed. Jesus not only was a good teacher, but he could also make sick people well!

Begin moving Jesus and his disciples out of the synagogue scene.

When worship time was over, Jesus and his disciples left the synagogue. It was time to go to Peter's home for Sabbath dinner.

Turn the synagogue scene around to the house side and set it on the left side of the underlay.

The disciples and Jesus looked forward to Sabbath dinner. Peter's mother-in-law was a good cook. She was glad to fix Sabbath dinner for Jesus, Peter, and their friends. After dinner there would be extra time to talk together, and many friends would stop by. The Sabbath day was a special day, not only for worship, but for spending time with friends.

Slowly move Jesus and the disciples toward the house scene.

Peter's house was not far from the synagogue.

Have Jesus and the disciples arrive at the house.

As they entered the house, they sensed something was wrong. The house was so quiet. Where was everyone? Why wasn't dinner ready? What had happened? Peter's mother-in-law usually greeted them by the door, but she wasn't there.

Point to Peter.

Peter began looking through the house. Where was his wife? Where was his mother-in-law?

Present the mat. Place it in the house scene and place Peter's mother-in-law on it.

Peter continued searching. Finally he found his mother-in-law. She was lying down on her bed. Now Peter was really concerned. His mother-in-law was usually not lying in bed during the day. Something was truly wrong.

Place Peter next to the mat.

As Peter came closer, he saw that his mother-in-law was very quiet. Her face was very flushed, and when he reached out to touch her, she was very warm. She had a fever!

Move Peter to Jesus.

Peter went to get Jesus. He was sure Jesus could help. Hadn't Jesus just healed the man in the synagogue? Hadn't Jesus turned water to wine at the wedding feast? Surely Jesus could help!

Move Peter and Jesus back to the mat.

Peter took Jesus to his mother-in-law.

Point to Jesus.

Jesus helped Peter's mother-in-law get up.

Put Peter's mother-in-law in an upright position.

All of a sudden the fever was gone! Her strength came back. She was all better.

Move the mother-in-law back to where the others are in the house scene.

Now she could do all the things she enjoyed doing to make Jesus, Peter, and their friends comfortable.

Point to all the figures.

Jesus had made Peter's mother-in-law better. What a happy afternoon everyone enjoyed!

Pause.

Jesus healed people's bodies and told them about God's love.

Pause and reflect on the whole scene.

Begin the wondering time.

I wonder what it was like to worship in a synagogue.

I wonder what everyone thought when the man called out, "Why are you bothering us, Jesus of Nazareth?" during the worship time.

I wonder how the people felt when Jesus healed the man.

I wonder how the man felt when Jesus healed him.

I wonder how Peter's mother-in-law felt when she was sick.

I wonder how she felt when Jesus made her better.

I wonder what Peter and the other disciples thought when Jesus made so many sick people well.

Return to the worship outline and continue.

20

Jesus Walks on Water

Scripture sources: Matthew 14:22–33; Mark 6:45–51;
  John 6:16–21
Materials:
  Figures of Jesus, Peter, and three disciples
  Blue underlay
  Green felt (8" x 22")
  Boat-shaped basket
  Tray to hold all the materials
Scripture to read: Matthew 14:22–33
Bible marker: A picture of the boat in the storm and
  Jesus reaching out to Peter to remind us of Jesus'
  power even over storms

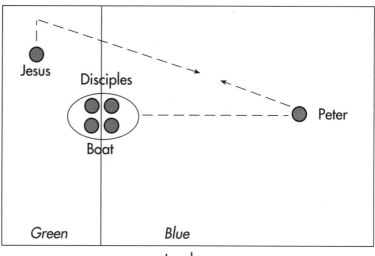

Carefully spread out the blue underlay. Add the green piece along the left edge. Present Jesus. Set him on the green part of the underlay at the near edge. With your hands go through the motions of taking, blessing, breaking, and giving.

Jesus had taken and blessed a little boy's lunch of five small loaves of bread and two fishes. Over five-thousand people had enough to eat.

Present the boat and set it on the underlay, half on the green and half on the blue.

The boat that had brought Jesus and his friends to the hillside was still there on the shore.

Present the disciples and place them in the boat.

Jesus told his disciples to get into the boat and return to the other side of the lake where they had come from that morning.

Move the boat so it is completely on the blue part. Point to Jesus.

Jesus stayed behind.

Indicate with a sweeping motion of your hand the crowd around Jesus.

The large crowd had heard Jesus teach and they had finished eating the bread and fish, so Jesus sent them home.

Pause. Move Jesus away from you on the green side of the underlay.

Now all alone, Jesus went into the hills to pray. He needed time to talk with God. For a long time Jesus stayed in the hills praying. The sun went down and nighttime came. Still Jesus talked with God.

Pause. Pick up the boat.

Out on the lake the disciples took their time. The day had been busy with many people. They had heard Jesus teach and had helped give the bread and fish to all the people. Now it was quiet, and they could rest and relax. It felt so good to be on the calm water, moving slowly in their boat. The sun was going down, and the sunset was beautiful.

Pause.

But as darkness came, the wind started blowing. The waves were no longer calm and gentle but grew bigger and bigger.

Begin rocking the boat back and forth.

It was very dark, and the strong wind was making big waves. The disciples were scared. They tried rowing harder but the waves were too big. They tried rowing to shore but the wind was blowing them in the other direction. What were they going to do?

Set the boat in the middle of the blue. Point to Jesus.	Jesus was still on shore but he noticed the wind. He saw the disciples struggling to row to shore.
Move Jesus toward the boat.	Jesus began walking toward the disciples. He walked right on top of the water!
Point to the disciples.	The disciples were terrified! Not only was there a storm on the lake but now something was coming toward them, walking on the water!
Point to Jesus.	Jesus said, "Don't be afraid! It is I, Jesus."
Point to Peter.	Peter called out, "Jesus, if it is really you, tell me to come to you, walking on the water."
Point to Jesus.	Jesus said, "Okay. It is I, Jesus. Come."
Take Peter from the boat and move him over the water toward Jesus.	Peter got out of the boat and began walking toward Jesus. Suddenly Peter remembered the wind and the waves; he became scared and started to sink. "Lord, save me!" he called out.
Point to Jesus.	Jesus reached out his hand and rescued Peter.
Place Jesus and Peter in the boat.	Together they climbed into the boat. As soon as Jesus was in the boat, the wind stopped blowing and the waves died down. The lake became quiet and calm again.
Point to the disciples.	The disciples were amazed. "Jesus really is the Son of God," they said to each other. "Even the wind calms down for Jesus."

Pause and reflect on the whole scene.

Begin the wondering time.

I wonder how the disciples felt in the storm.

I wonder what it was like to hear Jesus call out to them in the storm.

I wonder why Peter could walk on the water at first but then he sank.

I wonder why Jesus wasn't afraid in the storm.

Return to the worship outline and continue.

21

Jesus Heals a Paralytic

Scripture sources: Mark 2:1–12; Matthew 9:1–8; Luke
   5:17–26
Materials:
   Figures of Jesus, paralyzed man, and four friends
   Green underlay
   Six 13" x 1" boards to make the roof
   Mat
   Platform
   Background of the inside of a house
   Background of the outside of a house
   Basket to hold figures
   Tray to hold materials
Scripture to read: Mark 2:1–5, 10–12
Bible marker: A picture of the man who was let down
   through the roof to remind us of how much the four
   friends loved the man and believed Jesus could heal him

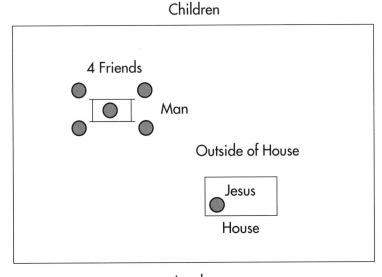

Carefully spread out the green underlay. Set the inside of the house background on the middle back of the underlay.

Present Jesus and place him in front of the house.

One day Jesus came back to his hometown.

News spread quickly that Jesus was home. Soon the whole house was full of people; even the doorways and windows were full of people.

Jesus talked to the people. He told them about God. He told them to love God and to love people.

Add the outside of the house background in front of the inside house background.

Present the mat and the man. Lay the man on the mat.

In that town lived a man who could not walk. All day long he had to lie on his mat because his legs were paralyzed.

Place the platform for the four friends near the man. One by one present the four friends and set them on the corners of the platform, with their arms facing in, as you say:

This man had four good friends. The friends heard that Jesus was in town so they came to get the man to take him to Jesus. They knew Jesus could help the man.

Lift the mat holding the man. Place the dowels in the arms of the four friends.

The friends picked up the man and his mat

Move the platform with the men next to the house.

and carried him to the house where Jesus was. But when they arrived at the house, they found that it was so full of people they could not get in. There were even people in the windows and outside the doors.

Lay the roof boards on the top of the house.

The four friends asked each other, "How are we going to get to see Jesus? There are too many people!" Then one of the men had an idea. They could get in through the roof!

Place the platform with the four friends and the man on the roof. Set it toward the back of the roof so you can remove the front boards.

Slowly and carefully the four friends carried the man up the outside stairs to the roof. Gently they laid him down. Then the friends began taking the roof apart!

Take two boards off the roof. Remove the outside of the house so the children can see the inside of the house.

When the hole in the roof was big enough, the friends slowly lowered the man on his mat until he was right in front of Jesus.

Place the man on his mat in front of Jesus.

Jesus saw how much the friends believed he could help the man. Jesus said to the man, "Your sins are forgiven."

With a sweeping motion, indicate a crowd around Jesus.

Some of the others around Jesus complained. "People can not forgive sins. Only God can forgive sins."

Point to Jesus.

Jesus knew what they said and what they thought. He said, "Why do you think like that? Is it easier to say 'Your sins are forgiven?' or 'Get up and walk?' To show you that I can forgive sins, I will heal this man."

Point to the man on the mat.

Jesus turned to the man on the mat and said, "Get up. Pick up your mat and go home!"

Set the man upright.

The man got up. He picked up his mat and walked away.

Indicate the crowd with a sweeping motion of your hands.

All the people were very surprised. They praised God for what they had seen.

Pause and reflect on the whole scene.

Begin the wondering time.

I wonder how the man felt to have to lie on his mat all day.

I wonder why the friends decided to help the paralyzed man.

I wonder how the friends felt when they got to the home where Jesus was and saw that it was full of people.

I wonder what the people in the house thought when the roof was taken away.

I wonder about Jesus, who can forgive sins and make people better.

I wonder whom we can bring to Jesus.

Return to the worship outline and continue.

22

Jesus Heals Ten Men

Scripture sources: Luke 17:11–19; Leviticus 14:1–32
Materials:
    Figures of Jesus and ten men
    Green underlay
    Beige felt road (6" x 36")
    Basket to hold figures
Scripture to read: Luke 17:11–19
Bible marker: A picture of one man saying "Thank you"
    to Jesus for healing him to remind us of the ten men
    Jesus healed and the one who said "thank you"

Children

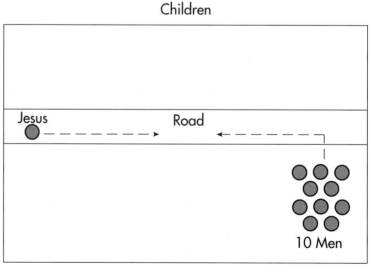

Leader

Carefully spread out the green underlay. Roll out the felt road as you say:

There was a road that went from Galilee to Jerusalem.

Present Jesus.

One day Jesus traveled this road as he was going to Jerusalem.

Set Jesus on the left end of the road.

Jesus was in a lonely place, far away from any village or town, far away from any other people.

Begin presenting the ten figures and placing them on the near right corner of the underlay.

Sometimes very sick people lived in these lonely places. They had a terrible disease that gave them bad sores on their bodies. Other people were so afraid of getting the sores too that they would not let the sick people live with their families but made them live in lonely places far away from the towns and villages. The sick people had to cry out, "Unclean, unclean," whenever they saw healthy people, and they had to stay far away from them.

Point to the ten figures.

The ten sick men saw Jesus on the road. They stayed far away from him and cried out, "Jesus, Jesus, please help us!"

Point to Jesus.

Jesus saw them. Jesus knew they had the bad sores. He knew they had to live in lonely places, away from their families. Jesus knew they did not have much to eat. Jesus knew everything about them.

Jesus called out to the ten men, "Go back to town. Go to the priest. Show him your arms and legs. Show him your faces."

Remove the men slowly, one by one, placing them back in the basket as you say:

The men started toward town. They were going to show the priest their arms and legs and faces. They hoped they could go home. As they were walking to town, they looked at their skin. Their skin was better! They were no longer sick! They were very excited.

Say with wonder in your voice:

The sores were gone! There weren't any on any of the men.

Continue removing the figures until the last one.

Now they could go back to their families. Now they could live in the villages and towns. Now they could live with healthy people.

Hold the last figure while you say:	One man remembered Jesus when he saw he was all better.
Place the one figure by Jesus.	One man came back to Jesus.
Have the man fall down before Jesus.	He fell on his face before Jesus and said, "Thank you!"
Point to Jesus.	Jesus said, "Were not ten men healed? Where are the nine others? Didn't they come back to say 'thank you'?"
Place the man on his feet.	Jesus said to the one man, "Rise up. Go home. Your faith has made you well!"
Move the man down the road.	The man was so happy that his sores were gone. Now he could go home to live with his family.

Jesus had made him well. He knew Jesus loved him very much.

Pause and reflect on the whole scene.

Begin the wondering time.

I wonder how it felt for the ten men to have bad sores on their skin.

I wonder how it felt to have to live in a lonely place outside of town.

I wonder what they thought when they saw Jesus coming.

I wonder how the men felt when they were healed.

I wonder why only one man came back to say "thank you."

I wonder how the families of the ten men felt to have their husbands and fathers back.

I wonder if the other nine were ever thankful.

I wonder if we should say "thank you" to God.

I wonder what we could say "thank you" to God for.

Spend a few minutes in prayer thanking God.

Return to the worship outline and continue.

23

Lost Coin

Scripture source: Luke 15:8–10
Materials:
  Felt figure of a woman
  Household objects: pictures of a table, chairs, a lamp, and a rug, all colored, covered with clear Con-Tact paper, and cut out (or cut objects out of felt)
  Green underlay
  Ten coins
  Gold box
Scripture to read: Luke 15:8–10
Bible marker: A picture of a woman to remind us of the woman who lost her coin and of the feast she had when she found it

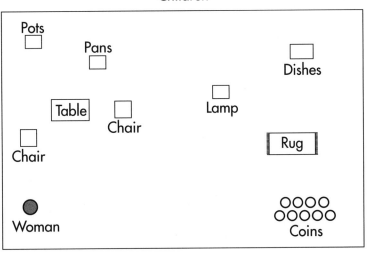

Children

Pots
Pans
Dishes
Table
Chair
Lamp
Chair
Rug
Woman
Coins

Leader

*Touch the gold box gently,
and with wonder say:*

I wonder if this is a parable. It might be. Parables are very precious, like gold, and this box is gold.

*Gently run your hand over
the lid.*

This looks like a present.

*Lift the box and admire it
like a present.*

Well, parables are like presents. They have already been given to us. We can't buy them or take them from someone. They are already ours.

*Trace the lid of the box
with your fingers.*

There's another reason why this might be a parable. It has a lid.

And sometimes parables seem to have lids on them. But when you lift the lid of a parable there is something very precious inside. I know. Let's take off the lid and see if this is a parable.

*Lift the lid and peek
inside. Put the lid back on
and move the box to your
side. Then open the lid
just enough to take out
the materials but not
enough for the children to
see inside. Take out the
underlay with wonder and
say:*

I wonder what this could be.

*Carefully spread out the
green underlay. Present
the household items and
place them on the
underlay. Try to hide one
coin under one of the
household items without
the children seeing you do
it.*

Jesus said such amazing things and did such wonderful things that people began to follow him. One day as they followed him he told this story:

*Present the woman. Place
her on the left side of the
underlay.*

Once there was a woman who had ten coins.

Present nine coins and add them to the near right corner of the underlay in two rows—five in one row and four in the second row.

But one day as she counted her coins,

Touch the coins as you count them.

"one, two, three, four, five, six, seven, eight, nine,"

Stop at the empty spot and point to it.

she noticed that one coin was missing.

Pause.

What was she to do now? One coin was missing! Where could her coin be?

Present the lamp.

The woman lit her lamp. She took her lamp and began to search her house.

She looked under everything. She grew tired looking for her coin but she did not give up. She kept looking and looking.

Carefully pick up each item in the house as you say:

She looked under the chair, under the table, under the dishes. She moved the pots and pans. She looked in the closets and under her bed. She kept looking and looking. She was tired and it was growing late, but still the woman continued to look for her coin. She looked under the rug, under everything, and into everything she could think of.

Pause.

Where can my coin be? Where else can I look for it? she wondered as she continued looking and looking.

Finally, pick up the item under which the coin is hidden.

At last she found her coin.

Place the coin in its spot in the row with the other coins.

Now she had ten coins.

Count the coins.

One, two, three, four, five, six, seven, eight, nine, and ten. Ten coins.

Point to the woman. She was so happy to have found her coin that she called all her friends and neighbors and had a great feast, a great celebration. "Rejoice with me. I have found my lost coin!" she said.

Pause and reflect on the whole scene.

Begin the wondering time.

I wonder how the woman felt when she lost her coin.

I wonder why the woman worked so hard to find one coin.

I wonder how her friends and family felt when the woman called them to a feast.

Point to the woman. I wonder who the woman really is.

Point to the coins. I wonder what these coins really are.

Indicate the whole scene. I wonder where this place might really be.

Return to the worship outline and continue.

24

Lost Son

Scripture source: Luke 15:11–32
Materials:
> Pictures of father, two sons, pigs, and bags of coins (2 fat bags and 2 flat ones), all colored, covered with clear Con-Tact paper, and cut out (or cut objects out of felt)
> Green underlay
> Brown felt (22" x 12") to cover 1/3 of the underlay
> Gold box

Scripture to read: Luke 15:11–24
Bible marker: A picture of a son coming home to his father to remind us of the lost son who returned to his father

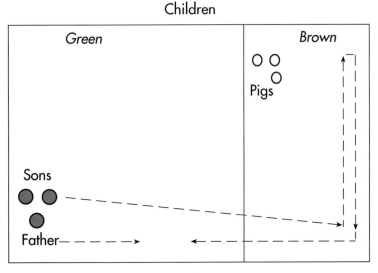

Touch the gold box gently, and with wonder say:

I wonder if this is a parable. It might be. Parables are very precious, like gold, and this box is gold.

Gently run your hand over the lid.

This looks like a present.

Lift the box and admire it like a present.

Well, parables are like presents. They have already been given to us. We can't buy them or take them from someone. They are already ours.

Trace the lid of the box with your fingers.

There's another reason why this might be a parable. It has a lid.

And sometimes parables seem to have lids on them. But when you lift the lid of a parable there is something very precious inside. I know. Let's take off the lid and see if this is a parable.

Lift the lid and peek inside. Put the lid back on and move the box to your side. Then open the lid just enough to take out the materials but not enough for the children to see inside. Take out the underlay with wonder and say:

I wonder what this could be.

Carefully spread out the green underlay.

Because Jesus said such amazing things and did such wonderful things, many people began to follow him. As they followed him he told them this story:

Add the man and his two sons to the near left corner as you say:

Once there was a man who had two sons. They lived at home with their father and helped care for the father's sheep and fields. The father was rich and had many servants to help his two boys do all the work on the farm.

Point to the youngest son.

The younger son thought and thought as he worked. He wondered, *Why do I work so hard? I would like to see how other people live and what they do. I wonder what it's like in the city. I wonder how it would be to leave this farm. Since part of this farm belongs to me, maybe I'll ask my father for my share.*

Pause.

The more he thought about these things, the more he wanted to leave. So one day he came to his father.

Move the youngest son next to the father.

"Father," he said. "I would like the money for my share of the farm. I want to leave here and see how other people live."

Place the fat bags of money on the underlay between the father and the son.

The father gave the youngest son his share of what the farm was worth.

Have the son take the bags and begin to move away.

One day this young man took his money, his clothes, and all he had and left his father and his brother.

Move the son slowly to the near right corner of the underlay.

Off he went to a distant country.

Pause.

People liked to be with the young man because he had a lot of money in his bags. He spent a coin here on a party, and two coins there on another party. There were always people around him to help him spend his money.

Replace the fat bags of money with the flat ones.

But the young man did no work. He never thought about putting money back into his bags. He just spent it, and, after awhile, he had no money left, no gold coins to spend.

"Let's have a party," the people around him said.

"I have no money, no gold coins," the young man said. "You pay for the party." But the others had nothing either, and one by one they left the young man until he was all alone.

Remove the flat bags.

What should I do now? wondered the youngest son.

Spread the brown material over part of the right side of the underlay.

Now he had no money and he had no friends. Then a very bad famine came. No rain fell, and no crops grew. There was no food.

Move the son slowly to the far right corner of the underlay.

The young man searched and searched for something to eat. Finally he decided to take a job

Add the pigs.

feeding pigs! The pigs had a lot to eat, but he was hungry. Nobody gave him anything to eat. He was so hungry he wanted to eat the food the pigs were eating!

Pause. Point to the father.

Back at home, the father waited and waited for his son who had been gone a long time. Each day the father looked down the road wondering if his son was coming back. But no son came.

Pause. Point to the youngest son.

One day, the young man thought, *Why am I sitting here in the pigpen starving to death? This is crazy. At my father's house everyone has enough to eat—even the servants. I am going home. I will tell my father that I am sorry I have sinned. I will tell him that I am not even worthy to be his son, and I will ask him to just make me a servant.* So the son got up and left the pigpen.

Move the son slowly across the underlay to the father, retracing the son's earlier path.

Slowly, he walked to his father's house. He was still a long way off when his father saw him coming.

Move the father quickly to the son.

His father saw his youngest son coming. He was so happy! He ran to meet him.

Have the father and son meet.

The father hugged and kissed his son. He was very happy to see him.

Point to the son.

The son said, "Father, I have sinned against God and you. I am not fit to be your son anymore."

Move the son and father home.

But the father called the servants. "Quickly," he said, "Bring a clean robe and put it on my son. Put a ring on his finger and shoes on his feet. Let's have a feast. My son, who I thought was dead, is alive. He was lost but now he's found."

And so the father had a great feast, a great celebration, because his son was home. The father said, "Rejoice with me. My lost son is found!"

Pause and reflect on the whole scene.

Begin the wondering time.

I wonder how the father felt when the son asked for his share of the farm.

I wonder how the son felt when he got all that money.

I wonder what the son was thinking as he left home.

I wonder what it is like to have no money, no friends, and no food.

I wonder what the son was thinking as he walked back home.

Point to the father.   I wonder who the father really is.

Point to the son.   I wonder if the son has a name.

Indicate the whole underlay.   I wonder where this place might really be.

I wonder about the stories with the lost coin and the lost son. I wonder what they mean.

Return to the worship outline and continue.

Lent Series for Year Five

25

Lazarus

Scripture source: John 11:1–44
Materials:
    Figures of Mary, Martha, Lazarus, and Jesus
    Purple felt underlay (18" x 72")
    Strip of white material (1" x 36")
    Tomb with door
    Purple basket (12" x 14") to hold materials
Scripture to read: John 11:1–2, 17, 38–44
Bible marker: A picture of Jesus, and Lazarus in his
    grave clothes to remind us of Jesus' power even over
    death

Children

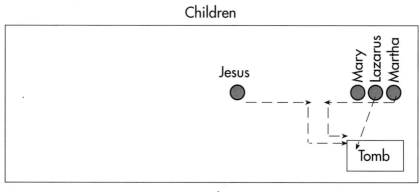

Leader

Carefully unroll the purple underlay. (Each of the six stories in this series uses about 12" of the underlay.)	Today is the first Sunday in Lent. Lent is the time we get ready to celebrate Easter. That is when God brought Jesus back to life. How do we get ready?
Pause.	One way to get ready is to think about some of the things Jesus said and did.
Pause.	Near Jerusalem was the town of Bethany. A brother and his two sisters, who were friends of Jesus, lived in Bethany.
Present Lazarus, Mary, and Martha. Set them on the far right end of the underlay.	Mary, Martha, and Lazarus loved Jesus very much. When Jesus passed through Bethany, he would stay with his good friends.
Point to Lazarus.	One day Lazarus became sick. Each day he grew more and more sick. His sisters were very concerned.
Point to Mary and Martha.	The sisters thought, *Where is Jesus? If he would come, he could make Lazarus better. Why isn't Jesus coming?* Finally they sent a message to Jesus.
Present Jesus and set him about 24" to the left of the three figures.	"Jesus," the messenger said, "your friend Lazarus is very, very sick."
Point to Mary, Martha, and Lazarus.	The friends waited and waited for Jesus. But Jesus took so long to come to Bethany that Lazarus died. Mary and Martha were very sad that their brother had died.
Present the white material.	Carefully Mary and Martha wrapped their brother's body in cloths and spices.
Wrap the material around the Lazarus figure.	Carefully they prepared Lazarus's body for burial in a tomb.
Present the tomb and place it on the underlay between the sisters and Jesus.	This is a tomb. It is a place to put the body of a person who has died.
Place Lazarus's body in the tomb and place the "door" in front.	The body of Lazarus was placed in the tomb and a stone was rolled in front of the door.
Pause. Indicate a crowd of people around Mary and Martha with a sweeping motion of the hand.	Many people loved Mary, Martha, and Lazarus. So, many people came to be with Mary and Martha in their sadness.

Point to Martha.	Then Martha heard that Jesus was coming.
Move Jesus a short distance toward the tomb scene. Move Martha until she meets him.	Martha hurried to meet Jesus. "Oh, Jesus," she said, "if you had been here my brother would not have died! But even now I know he will rise again on the last day."
Point to Jesus.	Jesus said, "I am the resurrection and the life. He who believes in me will live. Do you believe this, Martha?"
Point to Martha.	"Oh, yes, Jesus. I believe," said Martha.
Move Martha and Jesus to the tomb. Add Mary.	When Jesus saw Mary, Martha, and all the others crying, Jesus cried, too.
Point to Jesus.	Jesus said, "Roll the stone away!"
Move the stone away from the front of the tomb.	Then Jesus looked up to heaven and said, "Thank you, Father, for hearing me."
Pause.	Jesus called in a loud voice, "Lazarus, come out!"
Remove Lazarus from the tomb.	And Lazarus came out of the tomb. Jesus said, "Take off the grave clothes and let him go!"
Slowly unwind the white cloth from around Lazarus. With wonder in your voice say:	Lazarus was alive! Jesus brought Lazarus to life again.

Pause and reflect on the whole scene.

Begin the wondering time.

I wonder how it felt to be special friends of Jesus.

I wonder how Mary and Martha felt when their brother became sick.

I wonder how they felt when Lazarus died.

I wonder how they felt when Jesus brought Lazarus back to life.

I wonder how Lazarus felt when Jesus brought him back to life.

I wonder how Jesus' bringing Lazarus to life again helps us get ready for Easter.

I wonder what else Jesus will do and say to help us get ready for Easter.

Return to the worship outline and continue.

26

Mary and Martha

Scripture source: Luke 10:38–42
Materials:
    Figures, underlay, and basket from previous story
    Small table
    Plates, cups, and other dishes
    Inside of a house background
    Small box to hold dishes
Scripture to read: Luke 10:38–42
Bible marker: A picture of Mary sitting, listening to Jesus, and Martha preparing food, to help us remember to listen to Jesus

Children

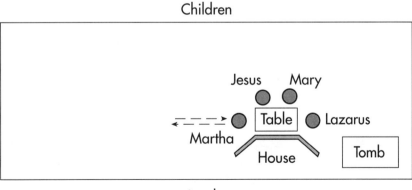

Leader

125

Carefully unroll the purple underlay.	Today is the second Sunday in Lent. Lent is the time we get ready to celebrate Easter. That is when God brought Jesus back to life. How do we get ready?
Pause.	One way to get ready is to think about some of the things Jesus said and did.
Present the tomb and set it on the far right of the underlay.	This is a tomb. This is where the sisters put Lazarus's body after he died.
Pause.	But Jesus brought Lazarus to life again.
Add the house background to the left of the tomb.	In the town of Bethany there was a home that Jesus enjoyed visiting.
Add Mary, Martha, and Lazarus to the scene.	It was the home of his friends Mary, Martha, and Lazarus.
Present Jesus.	Every time Jesus passed through Bethany, he stopped to visit Mary, Martha, and Lazarus.
Add Jesus to the scene.	Jesus loved Mary, Martha, and Lazarus. He enjoyed staying at their home. They talked and laughed and ate together. They enjoyed each other's company. Mary, Martha, and Lazarus loved Jesus very much.
Add the table to the scene.	One day Jesus and his disciples came to the village of Bethany. They stopped at Mary, Martha, and Lazarus's home. Now sixteen people needed to be fed: Jesus and his twelve disciples, plus Mary, Martha, and Lazarus.
Point to Martha.	There was so much to do. Martha was very busy.
Move Martha back and forth from just outside the house scene to in front of the house scene. Each time she comes back to the table, place another plate or cup or dish on the table.	Martha hurried and scurried. There was so much food to prepare. There was bread to bake; fruit to wash; and a salad to make. How would she get it all done?

And she wanted it to taste good and look nice because Jesus and his twelve disciples were there! Martha worried as she worked. Would there be enough food? Would it taste good? Would Jesus and his friends be pleased? |
| *Move Mary next to Jesus.* | As Martha hurried and scurried, fixing the food and carrying it to the table, she realized she was doing all the work by herself. *Where is Mary? Where is my sister?* Martha wondered. *Why isn't Mary helping me?* she thought to herself. |
| *Move Martha to the scene.* | The next time Martha brought some food to the table, she saw Mary. |

Point to Mary. Mary wasn't helping her because Mary was sitting by Jesus. Unlike Martha, Mary wasn't hot and sweaty or worried. Mary was calm and peaceful, listening to Jesus. *This isn't fair, Mary needs to help, too,* thought Martha.

Move Martha next to Jesus. So Martha went to Jesus and said, "Jesus, don't you care that my sister has left me to do all the work by myself? Tell her to help me!"

Point to Jesus. Jesus looked at Martha and said, "Martha, Martha, you are so worried and upset about the dinner and getting it ready. But only one thing is important. Mary has discovered it. She has been listening to me. Mary has chosen what is better, and I won't tell her to stop listening to me."

Pause and reflect on the whole scene.

Begin the wondering time.

I wonder what it was like for Mary, Martha, and Lazarus to have Jesus come to their home.

I wonder why Martha was so busy preparing the food.

I wonder why Mary chose to listen to Jesus.

I wonder what Martha thought after Jesus told her Mary had chosen the better thing.

I wonder what we would do to get ready for Jesus.

I wonder what would be good choices for us.

I wonder how this story helps us get ready for Easter.

I wonder what else Jesus will do or say to help us get ready for Easter.

Return to the worship outline and continue.

27

The Rich Man

Scripture sources: Mark 10:17–27; Matthew 19:16–30;
   Luke 18:18–30
Materials:
   Figures, underlay, and basket from previous stories
   Figure of a man
   Beige felt road (6" x 12")
Scripture to read: Mark 10:17–22
Bible marker: A picture of the rich man who asked
   Jesus a question and went away sad because he was
   not willing to give away his riches to follow Jesus

Children

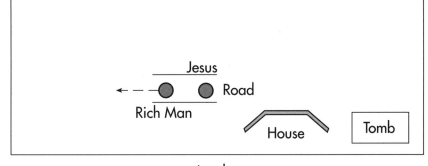

Leader

Carefully unroll the purple underlay.	Today is the third Sunday in Lent. Lent is the time we get ready to celebrate Easter. That is when God brought Jesus back to life. How do we get ready?
Pause.	One way to get ready is to think about some of the things Jesus said and did.
Present the tomb and set it on the far right of the underlay.	This is a tomb. This is where the sisters put Lazarus's body after he died.

Lay the cloth used to wrap Lazarus next to the tomb.

But Jesus brought Lazarus to life again.

Place the house scene to the left of the tomb.

This is the home of Mary, Martha, and Lazarus. One time when Jesus stopped here, Mary sat at Jesus' feet and listened to Jesus.

Carefully spread out the road to the left of the house scene.

This is the road that goes from Bethany to Jerusalem.

Present Jesus.

Jesus left Bethany and was going toward Jerusalem.

Set Jesus on the road. Present the rich man.

As Jesus was traveling, a man ran up to him. Now this man was very rich. He had gold and jewels and fine clothes. He had a big house and many servants.

Set the rich man next to Jesus.

This rich man had a question to ask Jesus. Even though he had a lot of money and could buy anything he wanted, something was not quite right. Something bothered this rich man. For a long time, he had thought and thought. This rich man had done everything right. But still something inside of him was not right. He had heard Jesus preach and teach. He had seen Jesus heal the sick. Maybe Jesus could help him. Maybe Jesus could answer his question.

I wonder what this rich man's question was?

Dialogue with the children about what the question might be that the rich man wanted to ask Jesus.

Pause.

Have the rich man fall down before Jesus and then set him upright again.

He fell on his knees before Jesus and said, "Good teacher, what can I *do* to have eternal life?"

Point to Jesus.

Jesus replied, "Why do you call me good? Only God is good."

Pause.

Jesus went on to say, "You know the commandments, the Ten Best Ways to Live: Do not murder. Be faithful in marriage. Do not steal. Do not tell lies about others. Do not cheat. Honor your father and mother."

Point to the man.

"Teacher," replied the rich man. "I have obeyed all these commandments since I was a boy. I have obeyed The Ten Best Ways to Live."

Point to Jesus.	Jesus looked closely at the rich man. Jesus loved the rich man. But Jesus said, "There is one thing more you need to do."
Point to the rich man.	The rich man listened eagerly. Now he would find out what he needed to *do* to feel good inside. Now he would find out what he needed to *do* to be given eternal life.
Point to Jesus. Say very slowly and with emphasis:	Jesus continued, "Sell everything that you have. Give the money to the poor, and then you will have riches in heaven. Then come, follow me."
Point to the rich man.	The rich man thought about his beautiful home, his jewels, all his money, and his beautiful clothes.
Pause.	He looked at Jesus again. Then the rich man's face grew sad.
Turn the rich man away from Jesus.	The rich man turned away from Jesus. He could not sell all his things. He could not give up all his money. He could not become poor and follow Jesus.
Move the rich man away from Jesus.	Slowly the rich man walked away from Jesus.

Pause and reflect on the whole scene.

Begin the wondering time.

I wonder how the rich man felt on his way to see Jesus.

I wonder how it feels to be so rich.

I wonder how the rich man felt after Jesus answered his question.

I wonder why the rich man could not sell all he had and give it to the poor.

I wonder how Jesus felt when the rich man turned away.

I wonder what was more important to the rich man than following Jesus.

I wonder if there is something that is more important to us than following Jesus.

I wonder how this story helps us get ready for Easter.

I wonder what more Jesus will say or do to help us get ready for Easter.

Return to the worship outline and continue.

28

Zacchaeus

Scripture source: Luke 19:1–10
Materials:
  Figures, underlay, and basket from previous stories
  Figures of three people
  Sycamore tree (with Zacchaeus figure cut out of the middle)
  Background scene of a city
Scripture to read: Luke 19:1–10
Bible marker: A picture of Zacchaeus in the tree to remind us of Jesus' visit with Zacchaeus and that Zacchaeus loved Jesus so much that he gave up his riches and helped the poor

Children

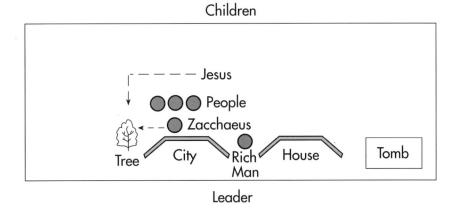

Leader

Carefully unroll the purple underlay.

Today is the fourth Sunday in Lent. Lent is the time we get ready to celebrate Easter. That is when God brought Jesus back to life. How do we get ready?

Pause.

One way to get ready is to think about some of the things Jesus said and did.

Present the tomb and set it on the far right of the underlay.

This is a tomb. This is where the sisters put Lazarus's body after he died.

Lay the cloth used to wrap Lazarus next to the tomb.

But Jesus brought Lazarus to life again.

Place the house scene to the left of the tomb.

This is the home of Mary, Martha, and Lazarus. One time when Jesus stopped here, Mary sat at Jesus' feet and listened to Jesus.

Present the rich man.

A rich man asked Jesus, "What can I *do* to have eternal life?" Jesus told him to sell all he had and give the money to the poor.

Set the rich man down to the left of the house scene.

But the rich man loved his riches more than Jesus. He walked away from Jesus.

Set the city scene on the underlay to the left of the rich man.

This is the city of Jericho.

Present Jesus. Place Jesus to the right of the city scene.

Jesus and his friends were on their way to Jericho.

Present Zacchaeus.

Zacchaeus was a tax collector who lived in Jericho. He was a Jew who collected money for the Romans. He was very wealthy. He had many fine clothes, a lovely, big home, and many servants.

But the people did not like Zacchaeus because he collected too much money from them. He cheated them and kept the extra money for himself. He had many nice things, but most of the people were poor.

Place Zacchaeus in the city scene.

One day Zacchaeus heard the people saying, "Jesus is coming! Jesus is coming!"

Add three people in front of Zacchaeus.

Now Zacchaeus had heard of Jesus' teaching about God's love and of Jesus' healing the sick. He wanted to see Jesus for himself.

But Zacchaeus had a problem. He wanted to see Jesus, but he was short and could not see over the crowd. What was he going to do?

Move Zacchaeus from the other figures and hurry him to the opposite edge of town from where Jesus enters.

Zacchaeus ran ahead of the people to where a wide-branching sycamore hung over the road.

Add the tree to the scene.

Zacchaeus climbed the tree and sat on a branch.

Place Zacchaeus in the tree.

Now he could see Jesus! Now the other people would not block his view!

Move Jesus and all the other figures close to the tree.

When Jesus came to the spot where Zacchaeus was, he stopped!

Move Jesus closer to the tree.

Zacchaeus wondered what would happen! Maybe Jesus would teach and he could hear!

Turn Jesus as if looking at Zacchaeus.

But Jesus looked up. Jesus looked right into Zacchaeus's eyes and said, "Zacchaeus, you come down immediately. I must go to your house today!"

Remove Zacchaeus from the tree. Place him next to Jesus.

Zacchaeus climbed down quickly! He was very excited that Jesus was coming to his house.

Remove one figure as you say:

The people grumbled. "Why is Jesus going to the home of Zacchaeus?"

Remove another figure as you say:

"Zacchaeus cheats."

Remove another figure as you say:

"Zacchaeus takes too much money."

But Zacchaeus and Jesus enjoyed a feast in Zacchaeus's home. They talked and ate. Jesus showed Zacchaeus that he loved and cared for him.

Point to Zacchaeus.

Finally Zacchaeus said, "I have so much and I have not been kind. Today I shall divide everything I have in half. Half I will give to the poor, to those who are in need. If I have cheated anyone, I will pay him back four times what I owe him. I will do it now. I will do it today!"

Add one figure as you say:

Zacchaeus gave this one some food.

Add one more figure as you say:

He gave another one a coat.

Add one more figure as you say:

To some he gave money. All the people he had cheated, he repaid.

Point to Jesus.

Jesus was very pleased. He said, "Zacchaeus, you are a son of Abraham. God loves you. Now both God and your neighbors are pleased with you. This is why God sent me to you. I have come to find and save the lost."

Pause and reflect on the whole scene.

Begin the wondering time.

I wonder how Zacchaeus felt when he was cheating the people.

I wonder why Zacchaeus wanted to see Jesus.

I wonder how Zacchaeus felt when the people said bad things about him and grumbled about what he did.

I wonder how Zacchaeus and the other people felt after Zacchaeus gave back all that money.

I wonder what Jesus meant when he said, "I came to find and save the lost."

I wonder about Zacchaeus who gave to the poor and about the rich man who could not give to the poor.

I wonder how this story helps us get ready for Easter.

I wonder what more Jesus will say or do to help us get ready for Easter.

Return to the worship outline and continue.

29

Mary

Scripture sources: John 12:1–8; Matthew 26:6–13; Mark 14:3–9

Materials:
  Figures, underlay, and basket from previous stories
  Figure of Simon
  Small perfume bottle

Scripture to read: John 12:1–4, 7–8; Matthew 26:10–13

Bible marker: A picture of Mary pouring the sweet-smelling perfume on Jesus' feet to remind us of how much Mary loved Jesus

Children

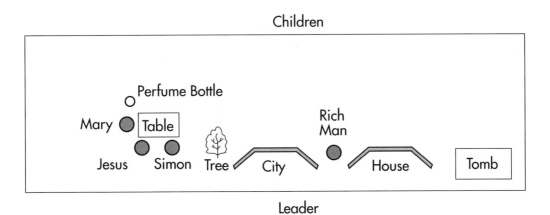

Leader

Carefully unroll the purple underlay.	Today is the fifth Sunday in Lent. Lent is the time we get ready to celebrate Easter. That is when God brought Jesus back to life. How do we get ready?
Pause.	One way to get ready is to think about some of the things Jesus said and did.
Present the tomb and set it on the far right of the underlay.	This is a tomb. This is where the sisters put Lazarus's body after he died.
Lay the cloth used to wrap Lazarus next to the tomb.	But Jesus brought Lazarus to life again.
Place the house scene to the left of the tomb.	This is the home of Mary, Martha, and Lazarus. One time when Jesus stopped here, Mary sat at Jesus' feet and listened to Jesus.
Present the rich man.	A rich man asked Jesus, "What can I *do* to have eternal life?" Jesus told him to sell all he had and give the money to the poor.
Set the rich man down to the left of the house scene.	But the rich man loved his riches more than he loved Jesus. He walked away from Jesus.
Set the city scene on the underlay to the left of the rich man. Add the tree to the scene.	Zacchaeus heard Jesus was coming so he climbed a tree to see Jesus. Jesus stopped right under the tree and called Zacchaeus by name. Jesus and Zacchaeus had a feast and then after they talked, Zacchaeus gave money back to the people he had cheated. He also gave to the poor.
Pause.	
Present Jesus and set him on the underlay to the left of the city scene.	Jesus was again in the village of Bethany where Mary, Martha, and Lazarus lived.
Present Simon. Place him next to Jesus.	This time Jesus was invited to the home of Simon for a feast, for a dinner given in Jesus' honor. It was a great celebration.
Add Lazarus to the scene.	Lazarus was there.
Add Martha to the scene.	Martha was there, too.
Add the table to the scene, placing it in front of Simon and Jesus.	Martha brought good things to eat to the table for Jesus and the other guests to enjoy. There was fruit, bread, and meat. There was water to drink.

Add the plates and/or other dishes used in the "Mary and Martha" story.

There was a lot of talking as people asked Jesus questions and listened to his answers.

Present Mary. Place her next to Jesus. Present the small perfume bottle.

Mary had a container of nard, a very expensive perfume. Mary took the perfume and poured it over Jesus' feet. The whole house was filled with the beautiful smell.

Put down the perfume bottle near the table.

Mary had long hair. She knelt down by Jesus and carefully wiped his feet with her hair.

Indicate the others with a motion of your hand around the table.

The others around the table were surprised and puzzled. *Why was Mary doing this? Did she know how expensive the perfume was?*

Some of the people started complaining. *Why was the perfume wasted when it could have been sold and the money given to the poor?*

Point to Mary.

Some of them turned to Mary and began to grumble against her.

Point to Jesus.

But Jesus said, "Be quiet! Leave her alone. Mary has done a beautiful thing. I will not always be here. She did what she could for me. She poured perfume on me to get my body ready for what is going to happen to me."

Pause.

Jesus continued, "I tell you that wherever the Good News about me is told, what Mary has done will also be told."

Pause and reflect on the whole scene.

Begin the wondering time.

I wonder how Lazarus felt to be with Jesus again.

I wonder what Martha was thinking as she served Jesus.

I wonder why Mary poured the perfume on Jesus' feet and then wiped his feet with her hair.

I wonder how we can show Jesus that we love him. *Talk with the children about what we can do to show our love for Jesus.*

I wonder how this story helps us get ready for Easter.

I wonder what more Jesus will say and do to help us get ready for Easter.

Return to the worship outline and continue.

30

Jesus Prays

Scripture sources: Matthew 26:36–46; Mark 14:32–42;
    Luke 22:39–46; John 18:1
Materials:
    Figures, underlay, and basket from previous stories
    Figures of Peter, James, and John
    Garden background
Scripture to read: Matthew 26:36–46
Bible marker: A picture of Jesus praying to remind us
    of the time Jesus was in the garden and talked with
    his heavenly Father

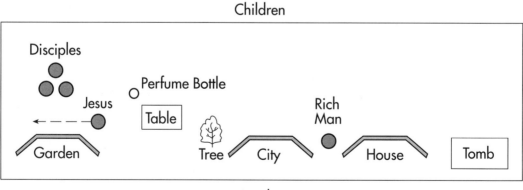

Carefully unroll the purple underlay.	Today is the sixth Sunday in Lent. Lent is the time we get ready to celebrate Easter. That is when God brought Jesus back to life. How do we get ready?
Pause.	One way to get ready is to think about some of the things Jesus said and did.
Present the tomb and set it on the far right of the underlay.	This is a tomb. This is where the sisters put Lazarus's body after he died.
Lay the cloth used to wrap Lazarus next to the tomb.	But Jesus brought Lazarus to life again.
Place the house scene to the left of the tomb.	This is the home of Mary, Martha, and Lazarus. One time when Jesus stopped here, Mary sat at Jesus' feet and listened to Jesus.
Present the rich man.	A rich man asked Jesus, "What can I *do* to have eternal life?" Jesus told him to sell all he had and give the money to the poor.
Set the rich man down to the left of the house scene.	But the rich man loved his riches more than he loved Jesus. He walked away from Jesus.
Set the city scene on the underlay to the left of the rich man. Add the tree to the scene.	Zacchaeus heard Jesus was coming so he climbed a tree to see Jesus. Jesus stopped right under the tree and called Zacchaeus by name. Jesus and Zacchaeus had a feast and then after they talked, Zacchaeus gave money back to the people he had cheated. He also gave to the poor.
Add the table to the left of the tree.	While Jesus was enjoying a feast at Simon's home, Mary came and poured expensive perfume over Jesus' feet and then wiped his feet with her hair.
Add the small perfume bottle to the scene. Present Jesus. Hold him while you say:	On the night before Jesus died, he celebrated the Passover with his disciples. The Passover meal helped God's people remember that the Angel of Death had "passed over" their homes and that God had led from Egypt through the waters to freedom.
Set Jesus down to the left of the table.	As they celebrated the Passover, Jesus said the words of the Passover in a new and different way.

Take an imaginary piece of bread, bless it with one hand, break it and give it to the disciples as you say:

Jesus took the bread, blessed it, broke it, and gave it to his disciples saying: "Take, eat; this is my body broken for you."

Take and hold an imaginary cup while you say:

Then Jesus took the cup, and when he had given thanks he gave it to the disciples, saying, "Drink of it, all of you. This is my blood shed for you.

"Do this in remembrance of me. For every time you eat this bread and drink this cup you are retelling the message of my death, that I have died for you. Do this until I come again."

Pause.

The disciples wondered, *What did Jesus mean by these words? What was going to happen to Jesus?*

Add the garden scene on the far left of the underlay behind Jesus.

This is the Garden of Gethsemane. After Jesus and his disciples had finished the Lord's Supper, they sang a hymn, and went to this garden.

As they entered the garden, Jesus told some of the disciples to sit down and wait while he went on ahead to pray.

Present Peter, James, and John. Place them in the middle of the garden scene.

Jesus took Peter, James, and John and went farther into the garden. Jesus left Peter, James, and John, telling them to stay awake and pray, while he went even farther into the garden.

Move Jesus to the far left front of the scene.

Now all alone, Jesus fell to the ground and prayed. "My Father! If it is possible, let this suffering be taken away from me. But I want your will, not mine!"

Pause. Point to Peter, James, and John.

Peter, James, and John heard Jesus say, "Pray. Stay awake with me!"

Have the three lie down one by one as you say:

But it was late and they were sleepy. One by one they fell asleep.

Have Jesus return to the three disciples.

Jesus went back to his three friends and found them fast asleep. "Peter," he called, "couldn't you even stay awake with me one hour? Keep alert and pray. Otherwise you will fall into temptation."

Move Jesus back to the far left of the scene.

Jesus left the three and prayed. "My Father! If this suffering cannot go away until I go through it, your will be done."

Move Jesus back to the three disciples.

Jesus returned to the three and found them still sleeping.

Move Jesus back to his praying place.

For the third time Jesus went back to his praying place. Again he said, "My Father, if this suffering cannot go away until I go through it, your will be done."

Pause.

An angel came to Jesus and gave him strength. Jesus continued in prayer with God. He prayed so earnestly that his sweat was like drops of blood falling to the ground.

Move Jesus back to the three disciples.

Now Jesus got up and returned to the disciples. They were still sleeping. Jesus said, "Are you still sleeping?"

Pause.

"Look, evil men are coming for me. Get up." Soldiers came and took Jesus. Jesus was arrested. Later he was nailed to a cross and died.

Say with wonder in your voice:

After three days, God brought Jesus back to life. Jesus is alive! God helped Jesus go through his suffering.

And now, Jesus is alive!

Pause and reflect on the whole scene.

Begin the wondering time.

I wonder what it was like to be with Jesus when he said the words of the Passover in a new way.

I wonder how the disciples felt when Jesus told them to stay awake and pray.

I wonder how they felt when they fell asleep and Jesus found them sleeping.

I wonder about Jesus who prayed so hard his sweat was like drops of blood.

I wonder if we can ask Jesus to go with us through difficult times.

I wonder how this story helps us to get ready for Easter.

I wonder what will happen to Jesus now.

Return to the worship outline and continue.

31

Raising a Widow's Son

Scripture source: Luke 7:11–17
Materials:
  Figures of Jesus, woman, her son, and four disciples
    (In this story use the disciples as the neighbors.)
  Purple underlay (72" x 18")
  Straw with heads of grain, if possible
  Purple basket (12" x 14") to hold all the materials
Scripture to read: Luke 7:11–17
Bible marker: A picture of Jesus and the man raised
  back to life to remind us that Jesus has power even
  over death

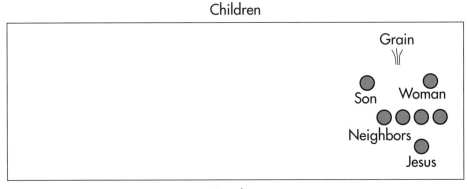

Children

Leader

Carefully unroll the purple underlay. (Each of the six stories in this series use about 12" of the underlay.)

Today is the first Sunday in Lent. Lent is the time we get ready to celebrate Easter. That is when God brought Jesus back to life. How do we get ready?

Pause.

One way to get ready is to think about some of the things Jesus said and did.

Present the woman. Set her on the far right.

In a little town called Nain, there lived a widow lady

Present and add the son.

and her only son. Together mother and son worked hard so they would have food to eat, clothes to wear, and a home to live in.

From early in the morning to late at night the mother and son worked in the fields. They hoed the ground, planted the seeds, and pulled the weeds.

Present the stalks of grain.

When the grain was ripe, they cut the stalks of grain, gathered them into bundles, let them dry, and then separated the grain from the chaff.

Place the stalks of grain on the underlay.

The grain was ground into flour and made into bread for the mother and son to eat.

Point to the mother and son.

Mother and son worked hard every day except the Sabbath day. That was the day to worship and rest. That was the day to remember all of God's gifts to them. It was the day to worship with the other people of the town of Nain.

Add the other figures to the scene.

Together with their neighbors, mother and son could take time to listen to God's Word and worship.

Pause.

But one day a sad thing happened.

Point to the son. Lay him down on the underlay.

The son became sick. Now the mother not only had all the work to do, but she also had to care for her son.

Point to the mother.

Lovingly she cared for her son. She helped him eat and drink. She fixed his favorite foods, hoping that would help. But nothing seemed to make her son feel better. Each day he became more sick.

Point to the others.

The neighbors helped. They did the outside work so the mother could care for her son. Sometimes they would bring in some food hoping it would help the son feel better.

Pause.

But nothing helped. Finally the son died.

Point to the mother.

Now the mother was left all alone. She was very sad.

Point to the others. Move them around the mother and son.

The neighbors felt sad, too. What was the mother to do now? Her husband had died. Now her son had died. Carefully they put the son's body in a coffin and began carrying it out of the town for burial.

Present Jesus. Set him next to the figures. Move the figures apart so Jesus can "see" the son.

Just then Jesus came to the town of Nain. As he entered the town, he was met by the mother and townspeople who were carrying the coffin that held the son's body.

Point to Jesus and then the mother.

Jesus saw the mother. She was crying. He knew her husband had died and now her only son had died and she was all alone. Jesus said, "Don't cry."

Move Jesus next to the son.

Jesus walked up to the coffin. He said, "Young man, get up!"

Set the son figure upright.

The son sat up and began talking.

Point to all the people.

Everyone was amazed. They began praising God saying, "A great prophet has appeared. God has come to help his people."

This news about Jesus spread everywhere.

Pause and reflect on the whole scene.

Begin the wondering time.

I wonder what it was like to have to work hard every day.

I wonder how it felt to be a family of just a mother and a son.

I wonder how the mother felt when her son died.

I wonder how she felt when Jesus brought her son back to life.

I wonder what the neighbors thought when Jesus brought the son back to life.

I wonder what the people meant when they said, "A great prophet has come. God has come to help his people."

I wonder how this story helps us get ready for Easter.

I wonder what else Jesus will do or say to help us get ready for Easter.

Return to the worship outline and continue.

32

Transfiguration

Scripture sources: Luke 9:22, 28–36; Matthew 16:21;
17:1–13; Mark 8:31–32; 9:2–13

Materials:

Figures, underlay, and basket from previous story

Figures of Peter, James, and John

Mountain

Scripture to read: Luke 9:28–36

Bible marker: A picture of Jesus, Moses, and Elijah on
the mountain with Peter, James, and John looking
on to remind us of the time Jesus shone and God
said, "This is my Son"

Children

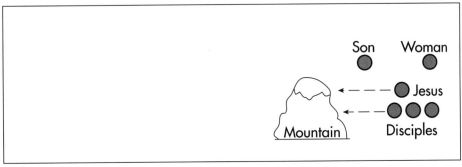

Leader

Carefully unroll the purple underlay. Today is the second Sunday in Lent. Lent is the time we get ready to celebrate Easter. That is when God brought Jesus back to life. How do we get ready?

Pause.   One way to get ready is to think about some of the things Jesus said and did.

Present Jesus.   Everywhere Jesus went, he told the people to love God and love each other. He healed the sick. He made the blind see, the deaf hear, and the lame walk again.

Set Jesus down on the far right of the underlay. Present the woman and her son.   Jesus also had the power to bring dead people back to life. In the town of Nain, Jesus raised the only son of a widowed mother.

Set the figures next to Jesus.

Move Jesus toward the left. Add Peter, James, and John next to Jesus.   As Jesus and the disciples walked along the road, Jesus began telling them that he was going to die, that terrible things were going to happen to him, but that in three days God would bring him back to life.

Point to the disciples.   The disciples were troubled. They wondered, *What did Jesus mean when he said terrible things would happen to him? Why was Jesus going to die? How could it be that Jesus would rise again in three days?* The disciples couldn't understand what Jesus was talking about.

Pause.   Jesus needed to pray, to talk with God.

Add the mountain to the scene to the left of the woman and her son.   One day Jesus took Peter, James, and John to a mountain.

Move the figures up the mountain.   Slowly they climbed to the top. They left the valley with its fields, went past the vineyards and pasture lands where sheep grazed, and continued climbing until they came to the bare brown rocks near the top.

If the mountain has enough space, lay the three disciples down to sleep.   Jesus went off by himself to talk with God. Peter, James, and John fell asleep. While they slept, something happened to Jesus.

Say with awe in your voice: Jesus changed. His face shone with glory. His clothing became dazzling white, whiter than any washing or bleach can make clothes here on earth.

Pause.   Suddenly Jesus wasn't alone anymore. Moses and Elijah joined Jesus and they talked about what was going to happen to Jesus, about his suffering, death, and rising again.

Point to the disciples. Set them upright.	The disciples woke up. They rubbed their eyes and looked around. Where was Jesus? Where had he gone? Then they saw him. They rubbed their eyes again. Jesus had changed! His face was glowing and his clothes were dazzling white! What had happened to Jesus while they slept? Who were the two other men with Jesus? The disciples were frightened.
Pause. If you desire, talk with the children about Moses and what he did.	And then Peter, James, and John recognized the two men. One was Moses, the law-giver.
	The other was Elijah, a prophet who spoke God's Word to the people.
Cover all the figures with your hands.	A cloud came and covered all of them. A voice from the cloud said, "This is my Son. I love him. Listen to him!"
Remove your hands.	Suddenly the cloud was gone. Moses and Elijah were gone. Jesus looked like he did before Peter, James, and John had fallen asleep.
Point to Jesus.	Jesus told the three not to tell anyone what had happened until after he rose again.
Point to Peter, James, and John.	Peter, James, and John listened to Jesus. They did not tell anyone what they had seen until Jesus rose again. But between them they often talked about what had happened on the mountaintop. They wondered what had happened to Jesus and why Moses and Elijah came and what Jesus meant when he said he would "rise again."

Pause and reflect on the whole scene.

Begin the wondering time.

I wonder how Peter, James, and John felt to be taken by Jesus up the mountain.

I wonder how Jesus felt when his face glowed and his clothes became dazzling white.

I wonder what Peter, James, and John were thinking when they woke up and saw Jesus.

I wonder what it was like to hear God's voice from the cloud.

I wonder how this story helps us get ready for Easter.

I wonder what else Jesus will do or say to help us get ready for Easter.

Return to the worship outline and continue.

33

Healing the Young Boy

Scripture sources: Luke 9:37–45; Matthew 17:14–21;
Mark 9:14–32
Materials:
Figures, underlay, and basket from previous stories
Figures of a man and a boy
Scripture to read: Luke 9:37–43
Bible marker: A picture of Jesus and the boy to remind
us that Jesus had the power to make the boy better

Children

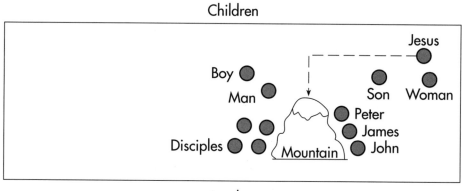

Leader

Carefully unroll the purple underlay.

Today is the third Sunday in Lent. Lent is the time we get ready to celebrate Easter. That is when God brought Jesus back to life again. How do we get ready?

Pause.

One way to get ready is to think about some of the things Jesus said and did.

Present Jesus.

Everywhere Jesus went, he told the people to love God and love each other. He healed the sick. He made the blind see, the deaf hear, and the lame walk again.

Set Jesus down on the far right of the underlay. Present the woman and her son.

Jesus also had the power to bring dead people back to life. In the town of Nain, Jesus raised the only son of a widowed mother.

Set the figures next to Jesus. Add the mountain to the left of the figures. Move Jesus to the base of the mountain.

Sometimes Jesus needed time to talk with God in prayer.

Present Peter, James, and John. Set them at the right side of the base of the mountain.

One time Jesus took Peter, James, and John with him to a mountain to pray. While they were on the mountain, Jesus' appearance changed. His face shone and his clothes became dazzling white. Moses and Elijah came and talked with Jesus. Then a voice from heaven said, "This is my Son. I love him. Listen to him!"

Point to Peter, James, and John.

Peter, James, and John wondered about what had happened on the mountain. But they told no one of their experience until after Jesus' resurrection.

Present and set four other disciple figures on the underlay to the left of the mountain. (Use the disciple figures that were used as neighbors in chapter 31.)

Now while Jesus, Peter, James, and John were on the mountain, the other disciples waited in the valley below.

Present and add the man and the boy figures. Set them near the disciples.

While they waited, a man came to them with his only child, a son.

Point to the boy.	The boy had a strange problem. He could not talk and sometimes he would have a seizure when he would fall on the ground, foam at the mouth, grind his teeth, and become very stiff.
Point to the father.	The father was very concerned. No one was able to make his son better. One day the father heard about Jesus. He heard that Jesus healed people. The man thought, *Jesus can make my son better.* So the father brought his son to the foot of the mountain to find Jesus.
Make a circling motion with your hand around the disciples, man, and boy.	Many people had gathered at the foot of the mountain. Some of them were talking and arguing with the disciples. The man and boy pushed their way through the crowd until they found the disciples. But Jesus was nowhere to be seen.
Point to the man and boy.	The father brought his son to the disciples and asked, "Where is Jesus? My son needs Jesus' help."
Point to the disciples.	They replied, "Jesus went up the mountain to talk with God in prayer."
Point to the man.	The father was disappointed. Jesus was gone. Now what could he do? Who would help his son? Then he had an idea! *Maybe the disciples could heal his son. The disciples were with Jesus all the time.* So the father said, "If Jesus isn't here, then will you, please, heal my son?"
Point to the disciples.	The disciples looked at one another. What were they to do? Jesus was gone but the son needed help and the father had asked them to heal his son. They looked at each other not really believing they could help. But they could try. They told the son, "Be healed." Nothing happened. "See," they said to each other, "we thought we couldn't help and we couldn't."
Move Jesus, Peter, James, and John to the left side of the mountain.	Just then Jesus, Peter, James, and John came down the mountain.
Move the man next to Jesus.	The father came to Jesus and said, "Teacher, I brought my son for you to heal. You were gone so I begged your disciples to heal my son, but they couldn't do it!"
Point to Jesus.	Jesus said to his disciples, "Oh, what tiny faith you have. How long do I need to be with you before you believe you can do such things?" Then Jesus turned to the father and said, "Bring the boy to me."

Move the boy next to Jesus.	Immediately the boy fell to the ground as he had done so many times before.
Point to the father.	The father said, "Please help us, Jesus, if you can."
Point to Jesus.	"What do you mean 'if you can'?" asked Jesus. "All things are possible for those who believe!"
Point to the father.	The father hastily said, "I do believe you can help my son. Help me to have even more faith!"
Turn Jesus to face the boy.	Jesus turned to the boy and said, "O demon of deafness and muteness, come out of this boy. Leave him alone."
Point to the boy.	The son was healed. He could talk and never again would he have a seizure. Jesus had healed him.
Set the man and boy apart from Jesus and the disciples.	Later when they were alone, the disciples asked Jesus, "Why couldn't we help the boy?"
Point to Jesus.	Jesus replied, "In order to help the son you needed to pray."

Pause and reflect on the whole scene.

Begin the wondering time.

I wonder what it was like to have a son who did those strange things.

I wonder how the boy felt when he did the strange things over which he had no control.

I wonder how the disciples felt when they could not heal the boy.

I wonder how the disciples felt when Jesus healed the boy.

I wonder what Jesus meant when he said, "You needed to pray."

I wonder who remembers what Jesus was doing on the mountain before the man and his son arrived.

I wonder how this story helps us get ready for Easter.

I wonder what else Jesus will do or say to help us get ready for Easter.

Return to the worship outline and continue.

34

Cleansing the Temple

Scripture sources: Matthew 21:1–13; Mark 11:1–11, 15–18; Luke 19:28–48; Exodus 11–13:2; Leviticus 1; Isaiah 56:7

Materials:

Figures, underlay, and basket from previous stories
Figures of sheep, doves, two men, Jesus on a donkey
Two small tables
Coins, three coats, and three felt palm leaves
Small box to hold coins and doves

Scripture to read: Matthew 21:6–13

Bible marker: A picture of Jesus sending the buyers and sellers out of the temple area to remind us that God's house is for prayer and worship

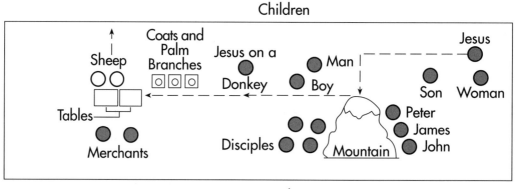

Children

Leader

Carefully unroll the purple underlay.	Today is the fourth Sunday in Lent. Lent is the time we get ready to celebrate Easter. That is when God brought Jesus back to life. How do we get ready?
Pause.	One way to get ready is to think about some of the things Jesus said and did.

Present Jesus.

Everywhere Jesus went, he told the people to love God and love each other. He healed the sick. He made the blind see, the deaf hear, and the lame walk again.

Set Jesus down on the far right of the underlay. Present the woman and her son.

Jesus also had the power to bring dead people back to life. In the town of Nain, Jesus raised the only son of a widowed mother.

Set the figures next to Jesus. Add the mountain to the left of the figures. Move Jesus to the base of the mountain.

Sometimes Jesus needed time to talk with God in prayer.

Present Peter, James, and John. Set them at the right side of the base of the mountain.

One time Jesus took Peter, James, and John with him to a mountain to pray. While they were on the mountain, Jesus' appearance changed. His face shone and his clothes became dazzling white. Moses and Elijah came and talked with Jesus. And a voice from heaven said, "This is my Son. I love him. Listen to him!"

Point to Peter, James, and John.

Peter, James, and John wondered about what had happened on the mountain. But they told no one of their experience until after Jesus' resurrection.

Present the man and boy. Set them to the left of the mountain.

In the valley below the mountain, a father and son came to find Jesus. The son couldn't talk and had seizures, so the father came to Jesus to have his son healed.

Add the four disciples next to the man and boy.

The disciples tried to heal the boy but failed.

Move Jesus, Peter, James, and John to the scene.

When Jesus came down from the mountain, he healed the boy.

Pause.

It was time to celebrate the Feast of the Passover. This was when God's people remembered how God had saved their firstborn sons. They had put blood on the sides and tops of their doorways as God had told them to do. Because they obeyed God, the Angel of Death had "passed over" their homes. Each year God's people traveled to Jerusalem to celebrate the Feast of the Passover, so Jesus and his disciples began their journey to Jerusalem. This year as Jesus entered Jerusalem, he rode on a donkey.

Present the figure of Jesus on a donkey. Set it to the left of the man and boy.

Make a road with the coats and palm branches (from where the donkey is to the left). Repeat this three times as you put down a coat and then a palm branch on top of the coat. Move Jesus-on-the-donkey figure over the coats and palm branches. Pause. Remove the figure.

The people spread their coats and palm branches on the road for Jesus and the donkey to walk over. They shouted, "Hosanna in the highest! Blessed is he who comes in the name of the Lord!"

People came from all over to Jerusalem to celebrate the Passover. They came to the temple to worship God, to give their offerings, and to bring an animal for a sacrifice.

Place the tables on the underlay to the left of the coat road.

Outside the temple was a large, open place called "Court of the Gentiles" where non-Jews could stand and worship.

Present the coins.

The temple priests accepted only the money used in Judea and some of the people came from other countries so they needed to exchange the money from their country for money from Judea.

Indicate the area around the tables with a sweeping motion of your hand.

This was the place where money changers exchanged the people's money for temple money.

Place the coins on a table and set a figure behind it.

But the money changers weren't always honest and fair. Sometimes they gave too little for what they took.

Pause.

The people also came to the temple to offer sacrifices—

Present the sheep. Set them in front of the second table.

a perfect year-old sheep

Present the doves. Set them on the table. Set a figure behind the table.

or a dove. People who came from far away couldn't carry their sacrifices with them so they bought them from the merchants in the Court of the Gentiles. Sometimes these merchants were unfair like the money changers. They charged too much for a sheep or dove or sold one that was not perfect.

Move Jesus next to the tables.

After Jesus rode on the donkey into Jerusalem, he came to the temple area. He saw all the people. He knew some of them had come to worship and pray.

Point to the sheep and doves.

He also heard all the noise—the people talking, the sheep bleating, and the doves cooing.

Point to the two figures behind the tables.

He knew that some of the money changers and merchants cheated.

Point to Jesus.

Jesus was sad as he looked over all the people and heard all the noise. He was sad that people cheated and robbed others. He was sad that people who wanted to pray and worship God at the temple could not.

Turn over the tables, spilling the coins and doves.

And so Jesus turned over the tables of the money changers and animal sellers.

Move the sheep to the edge of the underlay near the children.

He drove the sheep out of the temple area.

Point to Jesus.

Jesus said, "It is written, 'My house will be called a house of prayer for all nations,' but you have turned it into a den for robbers."

Pause and reflect on the whole scene.

Begin the wondering time.

I wonder why Jesus rode into Jerusalem on a donkey and not on a horse.

I wonder why the people spread their coats and palm branches on the path for the donkey to walk on.

I wonder how the people felt as they called out "hosanna in the highest."

I wonder how the people who came to worship and pray felt when their place to worship was filled with merchants, animals, and noise.

I wonder how the merchants and money changers felt when Jesus overturned their tables and spilled their money.

I wonder how the worshipers felt.

I wonder how this story helps us get ready for Easter.

I wonder what else Jesus will do or say to help us get ready for Easter.

Return to the worship outline and continue.

35

Widow's Mite

Scripture sources: Luke 20:1; 21:1–4; Mark 12:41–44
Materials:
    Figures, underlay, and basket from previous stories
    Figure of a woman
    An offering box and two small coins
Scripture to read: Luke 21:1–4
Bible marker: A picture of the widow giving her two
    coins to remind us that she gave everything she had

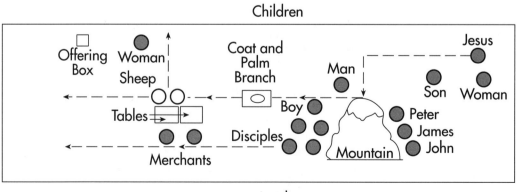

Carefully unroll the purple underlay.	Today is the fifth Sunday in Lent. Lent is the time we get ready to celebrate Easter. That is when God brought Jesus back to life. How do we get ready?
Pause.	One way to get ready is to think about some of the things Jesus said and did.
Present Jesus.	Everywhere Jesus went, he told the people to love God and love each other. He healed the sick. He made the blind see, the deaf hear, and the lame walk again.
Set Jesus down on the far right of the underlay. Present the woman and her son.	Jesus also had the power to bring dead people back to life. In the town of Nain, Jesus raised the only son of a widowed mother.
Set the figures next to Jesus. Add the mountain to the left of the figures. Move Jesus to the base of the mountain.	Sometimes Jesus needed time to talk with God in prayer.
Present Peter, James, and John. Set them at the right side of the base of the mountain.	One time Jesus took Peter, James, and John with him to a mountain to pray. While they were on the mountain, Jesus' appearance changed. His face shone and his clothes became dazzling white. Moses and Elijah came and talked with Jesus. And a voice from heaven said, "This is my Son. I love him. Listen to him!"
Point to Peter, James, and John.	Peter, James, and John wondered about what had happened on the mountain. But they told no one of their experience until after Jesus' resurrection.
Present the man and boy. Set them to the left of the mountain.	In the valley below the mountain, a father and son came to find Jesus. The son couldn't talk and had seizures, so the father came to Jesus to have his son healed.
Add four disciples next to the man and boy.	The disciples tried to heal the boy but failed.
Move Jesus, Peter, James, and John to the scene.	When Jesus came down from the mountain, he healed the boy.
Pause.	It was time to celebrate the Feast of the Passover. This year Jesus rode on a donkey into Jerusalem as the people spread their coats and palm branches on the road.

Place one coat and one palm branch on the underlay as you say:

"Hosanna in the highest! Blessed is he who comes in the name of the Lord!"

Add the tables, animals, coins, and merchants to the left of the coat and palm branch. Move Jesus to the temple area.

Jesus went into the temple area. He was sad when he heard all the noise and saw the money changers and merchants cheating those who came to worship and pray.

Overturn the tables.

Jesus overturned the tables and drove out the animals, money changers, and merchants, saying, "My house is a house of prayer for all nations!"

Pause.

Later in the week, Jesus was back in the temple.

Move Jesus to the left of the tables. Add the disciples.

This time Jesus and his disciples went farther into the temple, into the Women's Court where Jewish men and women could go to pray and worship. Jesus and his disciples sat on the steps watching the people come and go.

Present and add the offering box on the edge near the children about 18" from the left edge of the underlay.

In the Women's Court were thirteen offering boxes shaped like trumpets standing on end where the people brought their gifts and offerings. Some people brought things; others brought money. If coins were put in the offering boxes, the coins would rattle all the way down to the bottom making a lot of noise. Everyone in the temple area would hear and notice who was giving the offering.

Some rich people liked to bring many coins and fine gifts. They would stand by the offering boxes and take a long time putting their gifts and money in. Everyone in the area would notice the big gift and say, "Look how much that person is giving. What a fine gift to the temple." But even though the rich people gave big gifts, they had a lot of money left to use for themselves.

Present the woman.

While Jesus and his disciples watched, a poor widow came into the temple. Her husband had died and she had to work very hard for the little money she had.

Place her next to the offering box.

This day as she went to the temple to pray and worship, she took *all* the money she had. She had no more money left.

Hold up the two coins.

Very quietly she slipped into the temple area and walked over to the offering boxes. She slipped her two small coins into the offering box.

Lay the two coins next to the woman. With a sweeping motion of the hand, indicate a group of people between Jesus, the disciples, and the offering box.

The people who saw the widow lady said, "What a small gift! She gave only two tiny coins that are not even worth one cent. Why did she even bother? What can anyone do with that small amount? She should have stayed home!"

Point to Jesus.

But Jesus said, "I tell you the truth, this poor widow put more into the offering box than all the others!"

Pause and reflect on the whole scene.

Begin the wondering time.

I wonder what Jesus meant when he said, "This poor widow put more into the offering box than all the others."

Expand the conversation to include times when, because we do not understand, we may be unkind to other children who give a small or inexpensive gift.

I wonder how this story helps us to understand how Jesus wants us to treat people.

Expand the conversation to include the idea that what may be a big sacrifice for one child may not seem so much to another.

I wonder how this story helps us get ready for Easter.

I wonder what else Jesus will do or say to help us get ready for Easter.

Return to the worship outline and continue.

After reading the Scripture together during the Bible reading time, talk with the children about what Jesus wants us to learn from this story.

36

Washing the Disciples' Feet

Scripture source: John 13:1–17
Materials:
    Figures, underlay, and basket from previous stories
    Figures of five more disciples
    Large table
    Basin and towel
Scripture to read: John 13:1, 4–5, 12–17
Bible marker: A picture of Jesus washing his disciples'
    feet to remind us that Jesus wants us all to help each
    other just as he helped others

Children

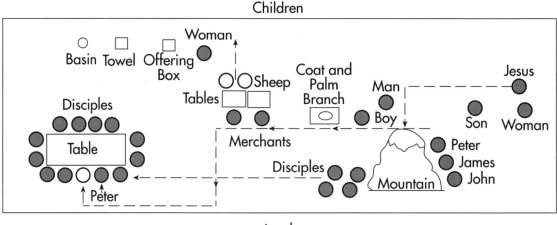

Leader

Carefully unroll the purple underlay.	Today is the last Sunday in Lent. Lent is the time we get ready to celebrate Easter. That is when God brought Jesus back to life. How do we get ready?
Pause.	One way to get ready is to think about some of the things Jesus said and did.
Present Jesus.	Everywhere Jesus went, he told the people to love God and love each other. He healed the sick. He made the blind see, the deaf hear, and the lame walk again.
Set Jesus down on the far right of the underlay. Present the woman and her son.	Jesus also had the power to bring dead people back to life. In the town of Nain, Jesus raised the only son of a widowed mother.
Set the figures next to Jesus. Add the mountain to the left of the figures. Move Jesus to the base of the mountain.	Sometimes Jesus needed time to talk with God in prayer.
Present Peter, James, and John. Set them at the right side of the base of the mountain.	One time Jesus took Peter, James, and John with him to a mountain to pray. While they were on the mountain, Jesus' appearance changed. His face shone and his clothes became dazzling white. Moses and Elijah came and talked with Jesus. And a voice from heaven said, "This is my Son. I love him. Listen to him!"
Point to Peter, James, and John.	Peter, James, and John wondered about what had happened on the mountain. But they told no one of their experience until after Jesus' resurrection.
Present the man and boy. Set them to the left of the mountain.	In the valley below the mountain, a father and son came to find Jesus. The son couldn't talk and had seizures, so the father came to Jesus to have his son healed.
Add four disciples to the left of the mountain.	The disciples tried to heal the boy but failed.
Move Jesus, Peter, James, and John to the scene.	When Jesus came down from the mountain, he healed the boy.
Pause.	It was time to celebrate the Feast of the Passover. This year Jesus rode on a donkey into Jerusalem as the people spread their coats and palm branches on the road.

Place one coat and one palm branch on the underlay as you say:

"Hosanna in the highest! Blessed is he who comes in the name of the Lord!"

Add the tables, animals, coins, and merchants to the left of the coat and palm branch. Add Jesus to the scene.

Jesus went into the temple area. He was sad when he heard all of the noise and saw the money changers and merchants cheating those who came to worship and pray.

Overturn the tables.

Jesus overturned the tables and drove out the animals, money changers, and merchants, saying "My house is a house of prayer for all nations!"

Add the offering box to the left of the tables.

Later in the week while Jesus watched the people in the temple giving their gifts, a rich man came and put a large amount into the offering box.

Set the woman next to the box.

A widow also came to the temple.

Show the two coins and lay them next to the woman.

Though she only put two small coins into the offering box, Jesus said she gave more than the rich man because she gave all she had. The rich man still had a lot of money left.

Pause.

Add the table to the far left middle of the underlay using the last 12".

This was the night to celebrate the Passover. Jesus had sent two disciples ahead of time to prepare the Passover meal in the upper room of a house.

Add Jesus to the scene behind the table. Place Peter on one side of Jesus and John on the other. Continue adding the other disciples until all are around the table.

Now Jesus and his twelve disciples gathered around the table to eat the Passover meal.

Point to Jesus.

But this evening during the meal Jesus got up.

Move Jesus to the children's side of the table. Add the basin and towel next to Jesus.

Jesus got a basin of water and a towel.

Point to the disciples.	The disciples began wondering, *What is Jesus doing? Why does he need the basin of water and towel? What is Jesus up to?*
Move Jesus, the basin, and the towel close to one of the disciples. (Begin with the disciple that is three away from Peter.)	Jesus knelt down, washed one of the disciples' feet, and then dried them with a towel.
Move Jesus to the next disciple.	Then Jesus moved to the next disciple and washed and dried his feet.
Move Jesus to the next disciple.	Jesus moved to the next disciple and washed and dried his feet.
Move Jesus again. He should be next to Peter.	Now Jesus was next to Peter and was preparing to wash Peter's feet.
Point to Peter.	Peter objected, "Oh, no!" he said to Jesus. "You shouldn't be washing our feet!"
Point to Jesus.	Jesus replied, "Peter, you don't understand what I'm doing, but someday you will."
Point to Peter.	Peter continued to protest. "No," he said. "I won't let you wash my feet."
Point to Jesus.	"But, Peter," Jesus replied, "if I don't wash your feet, you can't be my partner."
Point to Peter.	Peter exclaimed, "Then wash my head and hands as well as my feet."
Point to Jesus.	Jesus answered, "Peter, one who has already taken a bath all over, now only needs to have his dusty feet washed. Now, Peter, you are clean."
Place the basin and towel on the front of the underlay. Move Jesus back to his place behind the table.	Jesus washed all of the disciples' feet and then returned to his place at the table. Jesus and the disciples celebrated the Feast of the Passover, sang a hymn, and went to the Mount of Olives. There, soldiers came and arrested Jesus. Then a terrible thing happened, Jesus died. But God raised Jesus to life on Easter Sunday morning.

Pause.   Lent is the time we get ready to celebrate Easter and Jesus' resurrection.

Pause and reflect on the whole scene.

Begin the wondering time.

I wonder what the disciples were thinking when Jesus began to wash their feet.

I wonder who would usually wash the guests' feet when they entered a home.

I wonder why Peter protested.

I wonder why Jesus washed his disciples' feet.

I wonder how this story helps us get ready for Easter.

I wonder how each one of the stories helped us get ready for Easter.

Review each story and what it helps us learn as we prepare to celebrate Easter.

Return to the worship outline and continue.

After reading the Scripture together during the Bible reading time, talk with the children about what Jesus wants us to learn from this story.

Part
Three

*Two
Prayer
Series*

Prayer Series for Younger Children

37

We Talk with God in Prayer

Scripture sources: Matthew 5:1–2; 6:5–15
Materials:
  Figures of Jesus, four adults, and two children
  Green underlay
  Mountain
  Tray to hold materials
Scripture to read: Matthew 6:9
Bible marker: A picture of Jesus praying to remind us
  that we can talk with God in prayer

Children

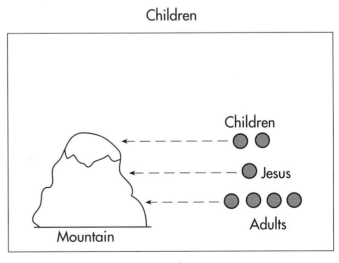

Leader

Carefully spread out the green underlay. Present Jesus and hold him as you say:

This is Jesus. Jesus told the people many things. He told them to love God and to love each other.

Put Jesus down on the underlay.

Wherever Jesus went, large crowds of people followed him.

Add an adult figure to the scene.

Daddies followed Jesus.

Add another adult.

Mommies followed Jesus.

Add another adult.

Grandpas followed Jesus.

Add another adult.

Grandmas followed Jesus.

Add the children.

Boys and girls followed Jesus. They all wanted to hear what Jesus had to say.

Point to Jesus.

They wanted to learn how to love God and how to love each other.

Present the mountain. Place it on the left side of the underlay.

Sometimes Jesus would go to the mountains.

Move Jesus to the mountain.

This day as Jesus went to the mountain, everyone followed.

Move each figure as you say:

The daddies followed Jesus to the mountain.

The mommies followed Jesus to the mountain.

The grandpas followed Jesus to the mountain.

The grandmas followed Jesus to the mountain.

The children followed Jesus to the mountain.

Indicate all the people with a sweeping motion of your hand.

All the people wanted to hear Jesus. What would Jesus tell them this time? What would Jesus say?

Put your index finger in front of your lips and say:

Sh-h-h! Everyone was quiet.

Point to each figure as you say:

The daddies were quiet.

The mommies were quiet.

The grandpas were quiet.

The grandmas were quiet.

The children were quiet.

Point to Jesus.

Jesus said, "When you pray, talk just to God. When you pray to God, praise God. When you pray to God, ask God for help every day. When you pray to God, thank God. When you pray, God will hear you. God always hears your prayers."

Nod your head in the affirmative and point to each figure as you say:

The daddies and mommies nodded their heads "yes." They would pray just to God. They would praise God. They would ask God for help every day. They would thank God. They knew God would hear them.

The grandpas and grandmas nodded their heads "Yes." They would pray just to God. They would praise God. They would ask God for help every day. They would thank God. They knew God would hear them.

The children nodded their heads "Yes." They would pray just to God. They would praise God. They would ask God for help every day. They would thank God. They knew God would hear them.

Indicate all the people with a sweeping motion of your hand.

Everyone was so glad they had come to hear Jesus. They were glad they had heard what Jesus said about talking with God in prayer.

Pause and reflect on the whole scene.

Begin the wondering time.

I wonder how the daddies, mommies, grandpas, grandmas, and children felt as they followed Jesus.

I wonder how the daddies, mommies, grandpas, grandmas, and children felt as they listened to Jesus.

I wonder what we can ask God to help us with.

I wonder what we can thank God for.

Return to the worship outline and continue.

38

We Talk with God at Home

Scripture sources: Exodus 2:1–4; 4:14; Numbers 26:59;
   Deuteronomy 6:1–9; Hebrews 11:23
Materials:
   Figures of three children and two adults
   Green underlay
   Background of the inside of a house
   Table and bed
   Tray to hold all materials
Scripture to read: Deuteronomy 6:4–7
Bible marker: A picture of a home to remind us that we
   can talk with God at home

Children

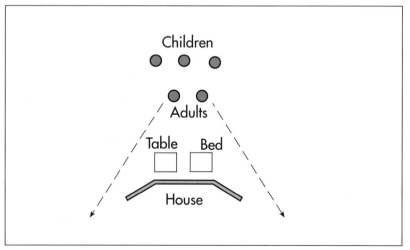

Leader

Carefully spread out the green underlay. Present the two adult figures.

A long, long time ago, way back in Bible times, there lived a man and a woman.

They loved God very much. They prayed to God and talked with God every day.

Put figures down in the middle of the underlay.

God put this man and woman together as a husband and wife. Now together they prayed and talked with God every day.

Set the house scene behind the figures. Present the bed and set it in the house scene.

They prayed when they got out of bed in the morning.

Present the table and set it in the house scene.

They prayed before they ate breakfast. They prayed before they ate lunch. They prayed before they ate their dinner.

Move the figures out of the house—one on one side and the other on the opposite side of the house scene.

They prayed during the day while they worked. God was with them all day. The husband had to work hard in the fields. The woman had to work hard, too. But they knew God was with them helping them.

Move the figures back to the house.

They prayed before they went to bed at night.

Pause.

This husband and wife loved God very much and wanted to talk with God.

Present one child.

One day a baby boy was born. The daddy and mommy named him Aaron. The daddy and mommy told Aaron about God. They taught Aaron to pray.

Add Aaron to the scene.

As Aaron grew, he prayed in the morning, at mealtimes, and at bedtime.

Present another child.

Soon another child was born. This time the baby was a girl and the daddy and mommy named her Miriam.

Add Miriam to the scene.

Now the daddy and mommy had two children to tell about God and God's love.

The daddy and mommy taught Aaron and Miriam to pray in the morning, at mealtimes, and at bedtime.

Present the third child.

In time one more baby came and they named him Moses.

Add Moses to the scene.   Now the daddy and mommy had three children to tell about God and his love.

Point to the bed.   Daddy and Mommy taught Aaron, Miriam, and Moses to pray when they got out of bed in the morning.

Point to the table.   The daddy and mommy taught Aaron, Miriam, and Moses to pray before breakfast and before lunch and before dinner.

Point to the bed.   They taught them to pray before they went to sleep at night.

Point to the children.   As Aaron, Miriam, and Moses grew older, they helped their parents with the work. The daddy and mommy knew God was with them all day and they told their children about God and prayed as they worked together.

Point to the parents.   The daddy and mommy did just as God had told them to. They taught their children about God at home, at work, in the morning, all day, and at night.

Aaron, Miriam, and Moses were happy to learn about God and to talk with God in prayer.

Pause and reflect on the whole scene.

Begin the wondering time.

I wonder if you remember when Aaron, Miriam, and Moses prayed.

I wonder if you remember where Aaron, Miriam, and Moses prayed.

I wonder when we can pray.

I wonder where we can pray.

I wonder how you feel to know you can talk with God in all places.

I wonder how you feel to know you can talk with God at all times.

Return to the worship outline and continue.

39

We Talk with God at Church

Scripture sources: Psalms 42:4; 122; 150

Materials:

    Figures of adults and children

    Green underlay

    Temple

    Scroll with Psalm 122:1 written on it

    Model or photograph of your church building

    Cars and people

    Pictures of a harp, horn, organ, and piano (covered with clear Con-Tact paper) or pictures of the instruments you use in your worship setting

    Bible

    Tray to hold materials

Scripture to read: Psalm 122:1

Bible marker: A picture of a church to remind us that we can pray in church

Children

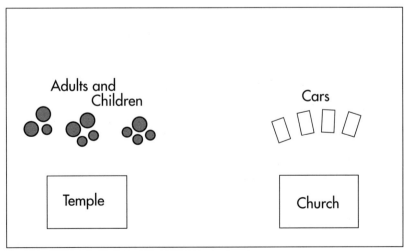

Leader

Carefully spread out the green underlay.

A long, long time ago, God's people worshiped in a place called a temple.

Present the temple. Set it on the left side of the underlay.

God's temple was a beautiful place. It had special furniture and lovely curtains.

Add the adults and children as you say:

The people walked to God's temple. The daddies walked. The mommies walked. The grandpas walked. The grandmas walked. The children walked.

Move all the figures closer to the temple.

The daddies, mommies, grandpas, grandmas, and children were happy. They were going to God's house to worship. They were going to God's house to sing and pray and tell God they loved him. Everyone was happy to be going to God's house!

Present the harp picture.

Some people played harps.

Present the horn picture.

Some people blew horns.

Present the scroll.

Inside the temple the daddies, mommies, grandpas, grandmas, and children listened to God's Word.

Untie the scroll.

A long time ago, God's Word was written on scrolls, and the priests read while the daddies, mommies, grandpas, grandmas, and children listened. They loved to hear God's Word.

Read the scroll.

The priest read, "I was glad when they said to me, 'Let us go to the house of the Lord.'"

Rewind and retie the scroll. Fold your hands.

The daddies, mommies, grandpas, grandmas, and children prayed. They said, "Thank you, God, for a beautiful temple where we can worship and pray."

Pause. Present the model or photograph of your church. Set it on the right side of the underlay.

Now we have this special house of God called _____ Church. It has _____ *(mention a physical attribute specific to your church, for example, stained-glass windows)*.

Add the cars and people as you say:

The mommies, daddies, grandpas, grandmas, and children ride to church in their cars.

Move the cars closer as you say:

The daddies, mommies, grandpas, grandmas, and children are happy. They are going to God's house to worship. They are going to God's house to sing and pray and tell God they love him.

Remove the figures from the cars and set them close to the church building.	They are going to God's house where they sing songs.
Present the organ picture.	Someone plays the organ.
Present the piano picture.	Someone plays the piano. The choir sings.
Present the Bible.	Inside the church the daddies, mommies, grandpas, grandmas, and children listen to God's Word, the Bible.
Open the Bible to Psalm 122:1.	The pastor reads from God's word while the daddies, mommies, grandpas, grandmas, and children listen. Sometimes they read along in their Bibles. Everyone loves to hear God's Word.
Read the Bible.	The pastor reads, "I was glad when they said to me, 'Let us go to the house of the Lord.'"
Close the Bible. Fold your hands.	The daddies, mommies, grandpas, grandmas, and children pray. They say, "Thank you, God, for a beautiful church where we can worship and pray."
	Pause and reflect on the whole scene.
	Begin the wondering time.
Point to the temple and the people around it.	I wonder how the daddies, mommies, grandpas, grandmas, and children felt as they walked to the temple.
	I wonder how they felt as they worshiped God.
	I wonder who remembers what the people of long ago did when they went to the temple.
Point to your church and the people around it.	I wonder how we feel as we go to church to worship God and pray.
	I wonder who remembers what we do at church.
	Let us all together say, "Thank you, God, for a beautiful church where we can worship and pray. Amen."
	Repeat the prayer a few times until all the children can recite it.
	Return to the worship outline and continue.

40

We Talk with God Everywhere

Scripture source: Acts 27; 28:1–16
Materials:
    Figures of Paul and two or three other adults
    Blue underlay
    Brown oval island (use an 8" x 11" piece of felt; round
      corners)
    Boat-shaped basket
    Tray to hold materials
Scripture to read: Acts 27:13–15, 21–26; 28:1
Bible marker: A picture of a boat in a storm to remind
    us of how Paul talked with God on a boat in the storm
    and that we can talk with God everywhere

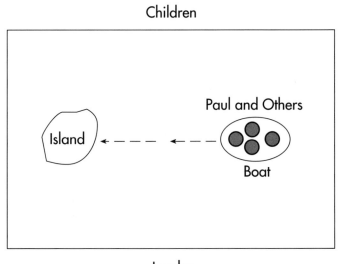

Carefully spread out the blue underlay. Present Paul.

Paul had gone to many cities and towns telling others about Jesus. Many, many people believed.

Return Paul to the tray. Present the boat.

Now Paul was being sent to the city of Rome. Rome was far away, and Paul needed to sail in a boat to get there.

Put the boat on the right side of the underlay. Place Paul in the boat. Add the other figures to the boat.

So Paul, some soldiers, and others got on the boat and started on their trip to Rome.

Move the boat slowly about 12" onto the underlay as you say:

Slowly, slowly the boat moved through the water. Since it was a sailboat it needed wind to move, and there was not much wind when Paul and the others left land.

Pause. Point to Paul.

At a harbor called Fair Havens, Paul said to the others, "We need to stay here. If we go on, we will have problems. We may lose the cargo, the ship, and even our lives!"

Point to the others.

But the others paid no attention to Paul. They wanted to continue sailing. When a gentle wind began to blow, the sailors decided to sail.

Pause.

But the wind grew stronger and stronger. It caught the boat and blew it out to sea.

Pick up the boat and move it back and forth as though the wind were tossing it.

The next day as the waves rose higher, the sailors began throwing the cargo overboard into the sea.

Holding the boat with one hand, use the other hand to indicate the motion of throwing things from the boat into the water.

The next day they threw the boat's tackle and everything else they could lay their hands on into the sea.

Move the boat back and forth as if driven by the wind and waves.

The storm continued for days. No one could see the sun or the stars, and no one ate anything.

Point to Paul.

Finally, Paul called everyone together and said, "Eat something. You need the strength. No one will die. Last night an angel of God came to me and said, 'Don't be afraid, Paul. You will get to Rome. No one will die but the ship will be wrecked!'" Then Paul took some food. He gave thanks to God. He broke a piece off and ate it. Everyone else ate, too.

Put the boat on the water. Add the brown felt island to the far left of the underlay.

The ship ran aground near an island. The front of the ship stuck in the sand while the back of the ship broke into pieces.

Move the figures from the boat to the island.

Those who could swim, swam to shore. Others grabbed pieces of wood from the ship to help keep them afloat until they got to shore.

Everyone was safe, just as Paul had said. The ship and cargo were lost, but not one person died.

Pause.

Paul and the others were safe because God had protected them. Paul prayed to God during the storm and God heard Paul's prayer.

Pause and reflect on the whole scene.

Begin the wondering time.

I wonder how Paul felt when he was in the boat.

I wonder how Paul felt during the storm.

I wonder how the others felt during the storm.

I wonder what Paul thought when the angel talked to him.

I wonder who remembers where Paul talked with God.

I wonder where we can talk with God.

Return to the worship outline and continue.

41

The Lord's Prayer

Scripture source: Matthew 6:5–13

Other sources: *52 Ways to Teach Children to Pray* by Nancy S. Williamson, pages 46 and 47

Materials:

White underlay (9" x 72")

Ten candle holders

Candles (one of each): white (taller than the others), blue, green, purple, brown, yellow, silver, black, red, gold, orange

4" x 6" cards with the words of the Lord's Prayer (from the King James Version) written on the front in the color to match the candle and the words to say for each candle written on the back (see pages 180–81)

Tray to hold the materials

Scripture to read: Matthew 6:5–13

Bible marker: A picture of Jesus praying to remind us that Jesus prayed and taught us to pray the Lord's Prayer

Children

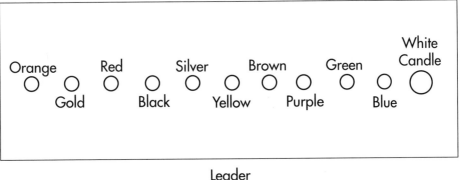

Leader

Carefully spread out the white underlay as you say:

Jesus taught his friends how to pray the following prayer.

Place the white candle on the right side of the underlay. Light it as you read the words on the card. Then set the card at the base of the candle. Do the same with each card and candle in turn.

1. **"Our Father"** (white candle; this should be the longest one used to show that God is supreme over all)—This first candle will represent God, who is light. How dark the world would be if this light should flicker or go out, but God has promised that he will never leave us alone.

2. **"Which art in heaven"** (blue)—The color blue reminds us of the blue heavens above us. God watches over us from heaven, but at the same time he is always with us wherever we go.

3. **"Hallowed be thy name"** (green)—Green is the most enduring of colors. The cedar and pine trees are green all year long. Green is the everlasting color. The name of God is everlasting, and it will endure forever. His name will be spoken and loved forever. He is holy, and we must keep his name holy.

4. **"Thy kingdom come"** (purple)—Purple is the royal color. The decorations of a throne are in this majestic color and so are the robes of a king. Our God is the King of Kings, and just as a king reigns over his subjects, God rules over the whole world. He wants to be Lord of our lives. We must give ourselves to God so that his kingdom can live in our hearts.

5. **"Thy will be done in earth, as it is in heaven"** (brown)—The color of the earth is brown. God made the earth and all its many people, so he knows what is best for this world. We need to let go of our selfishness and let God do his will in everything.

6. **"Give us this day our daily bread"** (yellow)—When God created the world, he also provided food for us. This is a prayer for our physical needs, and the yellow candle represents the grain that makes our bread. We need to bring our specific needs before him and believe his promises that he will hear and answer.

7. **"Forgive us our debts, as we forgive our debtors"** (silver)—The color silver represents the coins we use to pay our debts. This phrase, however, also refers to spiritual

debts and debts against our fellow man. We need to grant
forgiveness to others so that we can receive the forgiveness
God has for us.

8. **"Lead us not into temptation"** (black)—If we yield
to temptation, it will lead us into the blackness of sin. The
Bible tells us the wages of sin is death. We need to pray every day that God will put his armor of protection around us
to fight against temptation.

9. **"But deliver us from evil"** (red)—If we do yield to
temptation, God offers deliverance from sin through his
Son. Jesus shed his blood when he died for us on the cross.
Red reminds us of the sacrifice he made so that we could
live, if we just believe in him and accept him as our Savior.

10. **"For thine is the kingdom, and the power"**
(gold)—God's heavenly kingdom will not need the light of
the sun or moon, because the Bible says the glory of God
gives it light. God has never-ending power to do all the
things we ask of him in prayer, if we trust and obey.

11. **"And the glory, for ever"** (orange)—Orange is the
dominant color in a glorious sunset, which reminds us of the
glory of God. The great painters of the Middle Ages colored
the flame in the "burning bush" orange, which in their day
was understood to stand for Jehovah. That flame also brings
light, which reminds us of our first candle.

Now we have all the symbols of the Lord's Prayer shining
before us. No prayer is so full of divine radiance as the Lord's
Prayer. Every time we pray it, may we think of all these wonderful truths about our Heavenly Father.*

*Talk about the different colors of the candles and what they stand
for in the Lord's Prayer.*

Close by repeating the Lord's Prayer together.

Return to the worship outline and continue.

*From Nancy S. Williamson, "The Lord's Prayer in Color," in *52 Ways to
Teach Children to Pray* (1991). Used by permission of Rainbow Publishers,
P.O. Box 261129, San Diego, CA 92196.

42

The Persistent Widow

Scripture source: Luke 18:1–8
Materials:
  Pictures of a man and a woman, colored, covered
    with clear Con-Tact paper, and cut out (or they
    may be made of felt)
  White underlay
  Gold box
Scripture to read: Luke 18:1–8
Bible marker: A picture of a woman to remind us of the
  parable Jesus told to help us remember to always
  pray and not to give up

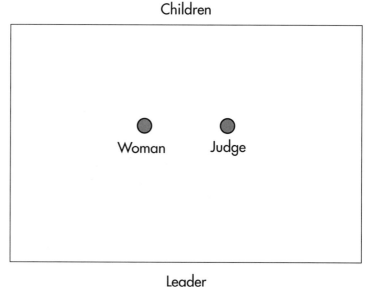

Touch the gold box gently, and with wonder say:

I wonder if this is a parable. It might be. Parables are very precious, like gold, and this box is gold.

Gently run your hand over the lid.

This looks like a present.

Lift the box and admire it like a present.

Well, parables are like presents. They have already been given to us. We can't buy them or take them from someone. They are already ours.

Trace the lid of the box with your fingers.

There's another reason why this might be a parable. It has a lid.

And sometimes parables seem to have lids on them. But when you lift the lid of a parable there is something very precious inside. I know. Let's take off the lid and see if this is a parable.

Lift the lid and peek inside. Put the lid back on and move the box to your side. Then open the lid just enough to take out the materials but not enough for the children to see inside. Take out the underlay with wonder and say:

I wonder what this could be.

Carefully spread out the white underlay.

I wonder why it is white.

Pause.

Jesus said such amazing things and did such wonderful things that many people began to follow him. As they followed him he taught them about praying.

Present the judge.

In a certain town there was a judge, a man who settled disagreements between people. He was an important man with great authority. People would come to the judge when others tried to take what belonged to them or when someone had harmed them.

Pause.

Now this judge did not believe in God. He also did not care what people thought about him.

Place the judge on the underlay.

He did not care about the needs of the people.

Present the woman.

In the same town lived a widow. Her husband had died and she was all alone. There was no close family to help her and someone was trying to take what little she had.

Place her on the underlay facing the judge.

This widow came to the judge to ask him to help her keep what was hers. "Sir," she said, "I need you to help me. The person who lives next to me is trying to take what is mine. Please tell him to leave me alone. Please tell him that this house and property are mine and he cannot take them from me."

Point to the judge.

But the judge did not care about the widow. He did not care that the man who lived next door to her was trying to take her home and land, so he ignored the widow. He did not help her at all.

Remove the woman from the underlay. Hold her as you say:

Sadly the widow went home. What was she to do? How was she going to live? If the man next door took her house and land she would have no place to go.

Place the woman next to the judge.

After a few days, the widow summoned up her courage and went back to the judge. "Sir," she said again, "I need your help. The person who lives next to me is trying to take what is mine. Please tell him to leave me alone. Please tell him that this house and property are mine and he cannot take them from me."

Remove the woman and hold her as you say:

But again the judge would not listen. He did not care about the widow. He did not care if she kept her home or land, so he ignored her. He did not help her at all.

Place the woman next to the judge.

After a few days, the widow summoned up her courage and went back to the judge. "Sir," she said again, "I need your help. The person who lives next to me is trying to take what is mine. Please tell him to leave me alone. Please tell him that this house and property are mine and he cannot take them from me."

Remove the woman and hold her as you say:

But again the judge would not listen. He did not care about the widow. He did not care if she kept her home or land, so he ignored her. He did not help her at all.

Place the woman on the underlay facing the judge but a little ways away.

Every few days, the widow returned to the judge. Finally the judge grew tired of her coming. She was so persistent! He was so tired of her bothering him that he decided to help her even though he did not care what happened to her. He thought, *I do not fear God or believe in God. I do not care what people think of me. But I am tired of being bothered so often. I will help this woman and she will stop coming. I will finally be rid of her.*

Move the woman closer to the judge.

The next time the widow came and said, "Sir, I need you to help me. The person who lives next to me is trying to take what is mine. Please tell him to leave me alone. Please tell him that this house and property are mine and he cannot take them from me."

Point to the judge.

The judge said, "Yes, lady, the home and land are yours. I will make it a law and put it in writing so the man who lives next to you will no longer try to take what is yours. Now stop bothering me!"

Pause and reflect on the whole scene.

Begin the wondering time.

I wonder who the widow really is.

I wonder who the judge really is.

I wonder why the widow was so persistent.

I wonder why the judge would not help the widow at first.

I wonder why the judge finally gave in and helped the widow.

I wonder how this story helps us understand more about praying to God.

Return to the worship outline and continue.

43

Jesus' Example of Prayer

Scripture sources: Matthew 6:5–15; 14:23; 15:36; 19:13–15; 26:26, 36–46; Mark 1:35; Luke 3:21; 5:16; 6:12; 11:1–13; 23:33–34

Materials:

  Figures of Jesus, a little boy, three children, and Jesus on a cross

  White underlay

  A 5" x 10" piece of blue felt and one of brown felt

  Five loaves and two fish, made of felt

  Mountain

  Small table

  Plate and chalice

  Small box to hold chalice, plate, loaves, and fish

  Basket to hold figures

  Tray to hold materials

Scripture to read: Luke 11:1–4

Bible marker: A picture of a boy and a girl praying to remind us that we can be like Jesus and talk with God in prayer

Children

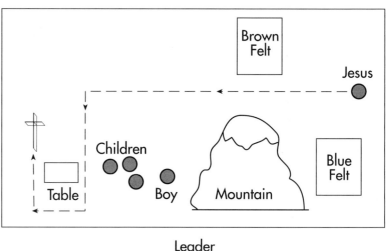

Leader

Carefully spread out the white underlay.	Today we are in the season of Easter. It is the time we think about Jesus and celebrate his resurrection.
	One way to celebrate that Jesus is alive is to talk with Jesus in prayer.
Present the Jesus figure.	Jesus prayed. Jesus can teach us to pray.
Place Jesus on the right side of the underlay near the middle.	The Bible tells us that Jesus was praying before he even began the work God had sent him to do.
Present the blue felt.	John, the Baptizer, was preaching and teaching at the Jordan River.
Place the blue felt on the right of the underlay at the edge near the leader.	Jesus went to the Jordan and was baptized by John. After his baptism, as he was praying, the heavens opened and the Holy Spirit, in the form of a dove, came down on Jesus and a voice said, "This is the Son I love."
	As Jesus began and continued his work, he needed time to talk with God, his heavenly Father.
	The Bible tells us that sometimes Jesus got up early to pray.
Present the mountain. Place it to the left of the blue felt.	Sometimes Jesus would climb a mountain to be alone and pray.
Present the brown felt and lay it on the underlay in front of the mountain.	Sometimes Jesus would go out into the wilderness by himself and pray.
Move Jesus toward the center of the underlay— moving him toward the left.	Sometimes Jesus prayed in front of many people. Once when great crowds followed Jesus to listen to Jesus teach, it grew late. The people were hungry and there was no food.
Present the little boy and the five loaves and two fish.	Jesus took a little boy's lunch of five loaves and two fish. He gave thanks to God for the food. When the disciples passed the food to the people, there was enough for everyone.
Set the little boy, the loaves, and the fish to the left of the mountain. Move Jesus a little to the left of the boy.	

Present the children. Place them next to Jesus.

Parents brought their children to Jesus. Jesus put his hands on the children and prayed.

Present the table. Set it to the left of the children. Move Jesus behind the table.

On the night that Jesus celebrated the Passover with his friends,

Present the plate and chalice and set them on the table.

Jesus prayed.

Pick up an imaginary loaf of bread with both hands. Put one hand over the other as in a blessing, break the imaginary loaf, and give it as you say:

Jesus took the bread, blessed it, broke it, and gave it to his friends.

Lift the chalice and hold it as you say:

Jesus took the cup, gave thanks, and gave the cup to his friends.

Set the chalice back on the table. Move Jesus to the left.

After the meal, Jesus and his friends went to the garden where Jesus prayed. Jesus asked God to take his suffering away but added, "Not my will but yours be done."

Later Jesus was arrested, tried, and then nailed to a cross.

Present the cross. Set it to the left of the table.

From the cross, Jesus again prayed. Jesus asked God to forgive all the people for what they were doing.

Pause and reflect on the whole scene.

Begin the wondering time.

Point to the mountain as you say:

I wonder how Jesus felt when he spent all night in prayer.

I wonder what Jesus and God talked about.

Point to the boy and the five loaves and two fish as you say:

I wonder what the people thought when they heard Jesus pray over the loaves and fish and then everyone had enough to eat.

*Point to the children as
you say:* I wonder how the children felt when Jesus prayed for them.

Review all the times Jesus prayed.

I wonder where we can pray.

I wonder what we can pray for.

I wonder when we can pray.

Return to the worship outline and continue.

44

The Pharisee and the Publican

Scripture source: Luke 18:9–14

Materials:

Pictures of two men, colored, covered with clear Con-Tact paper, and cut out (or make figures of felt)

White underlay

Gold box

Picture of the temple, covered with clear Con-Tact paper (or use a square of gold felt)

Scripture to read: Luke 18:9–14

Bible marker: A picture of the Pharisee and publican to remind us to be humble when we pray

Children

🔵 Publican

🔵 Pharisee

Temple

Leader

Touch the gold box gently, and with wonder say:

I wonder if this is a parable. It might be. Parables are very precious, like gold, and this box is gold.

Gently run your hand over the lid.

This looks like a present.

Lift the box and admire it like a present.

Well, parables are like presents. They have already been given to us. We can't buy them or take them from someone. They are already ours.

Trace the lid of the box with your fingers.

There's another reason why this might be a parable. It has a lid.

And sometimes parables seem to have lids on them. But when you lift the lid of a parable there is something very precious inside. I know. Let's take off the lid and see if this is a parable.

Lift the lid and peek inside. Put the lid back on and move the box to your side. Then open the lid just enough to take out the materials but not enough for the children to see inside. Take out the underlay with wonder and say:

I wonder what this could be.

Carefully spread out the white underlay.

I wonder why it is white.

Pause.

Jesus said such amazing things and did such wonderful things that many people began to follow him. As they followed him he taught them about praying.

Present the temple. Place it in the middle of the underlay.

This is the temple. It is a special place where people can meet and talk with God, a special place where people can pray.

There were special times when people could go to the temple to pray. There were the morning and evening prayers. These were times when sacrifices were also made. But people could also go to the temple at any time and say their prayers.

Present the Pharisee and place him right in the center front of the temple.

Once a Pharisee

Present the publican and place him in the left corner of the underlay.

and a publican, or tax collector, came to the temple to pray.

Pick up the Pharisee and hold him as you say:

Pharisees were very proud. They were men who tried to please God by keeping every rule in God's law. They even made up extra rules to God's law. They kept these rules and insisted that everyone else keep these rules, too. They had rules on what to eat and how to eat it; rules on how to wash the dishes; rules on what to do and not do on the Lord's Day. Their list of rules was very long. They even wore special clothes so everyone would know they were Pharisees.

Place the Pharisee back on the underlay.

Now one day this Pharisee came to the temple to pray. He was so proud of what he did that he stood up straight and tall and told God all about himself.

Fold your hands and look up as you say proudly:

He said, "God, I thank you that I am so good. I am so much better than others. I don't steal or take what belongs to someone else. I do nothing evil or wrong. I do not lie with another man's wife. I do not even think about doing that. I fast two times a week so I can pray better. I give one-tenth of all my income to God. Oh, I am so good. See that publican, that tax collector, that sinner over in the corner? I am not at all like him. I am so much better.

Pause. Hold the publican as you say:

A publican had also come into the temple to pray. Publicans were tax collectors. They took money from the people and gave it to the Roman government. They were hated by all the people because they usually took too much money and kept the extra for themselves.

Pause.

This publican stood way off in a corner of the temple.

Slap your chest with your free hand to show the children how it is done.

He beat his chest with his hands to show how sorry he was.

Place the publican back on the underlay. Fold your hands and bow your head as you say very humbly:

The publican stood way off in a corner and prayed. "Dear God, please have mercy on me, a sinner. I am so sorry for all the wrongs I have done and thought and said. Please forgive me."

Pause.

Point to the publican.

Jesus, who told this story, added, "God forgave this publican for his sin because he humbled himself in prayer before God."

Pause and reflect on the whole scene.

Begin the wondering time.

I wonder why the Pharisee was so proud.

I wonder why the publican was so humble.

I wonder who the Pharisee really is.

I wonder who the publican really is.

I wonder how God wants us to pray.

Return to the worship outline and continue.

Part Four

Stories from
the Book of Acts

45

Stephen

Scripture source: Acts 6, 7, 8:1–3
Materials:
    Figures of Stephen, Peter, John, and two men
    Green underlay
    Small stones
    Basket to hold materials
Scripture to read: Acts 6:5a, 8, 9b–15; 7:54–59
Bible marker: A picture of Stephen telling others about
    Jesus

Children

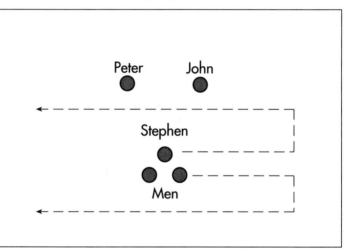

Leader

Carefully spread out the green underlay.

Today we are in the season of Pentecost. It is the time when we learn about more and more people believing in Jesus.

Present Peter and John.

Peter, John, and the other apostles preached and taught about Jesus. When Peter preached at Pentecost, three thousand people believed in Jesus. Later when the lame man was healed, many more believed and now there were more than five thousand people who believed in Jesus.

Set Peter and John on the middle of the underlay.

Peter, John, and the other apostles told everyone who would listen about Jesus. Every day more and more believed. Some of these new believers were poor and had no one except other believers to care for them. But when the apostles took time to care for the poor people, they had no time to go out and tell others about Jesus. The apostles wanted time to preach and teach, so they decided to choose seven men to take care of the poor people.

Indicate with a sweeping motion of the hand a large crowd around Peter and John.

The believers gathered to pray and ask God for help in choosing seven men who were filled with the Holy Spirit and had great faith.

Present Stephen.

Stephen was one of the seven men. Stephen's faith was strong and he was filled with the Holy Spirit. He would do a good job helping the poor.

Set Stephen on the underlay. Put Peter and John back in the basket.

Stephen did a good job of helping the poor. He made sure they had food to eat, clothes to wear, and warm homes to live in.

Pause.

But Stephen also had time to preach and teach. He told about Jesus to all who would listen. He even did amazing miracles. Some people did not like Stephen's preaching and miracle working.

Add the two men.

Some men began to argue with Stephen. They persuaded others to join them.

Point to Stephen.

But Stephen was such a wise and good man that no one could find anything wrong with him. They found some wicked men to lie about Stephen. They said he cursed Moses and God. They stirred up the people against Stephen so much that the Jewish leaders arrested him. They took him to the Council where the Jewish leaders met to decide what to do.

Move Stephen and the two men to the right of the underlay.

The wicked men continued to turn people against Stephen. They said, "This man says terrible things about the temple, God's house, and about God's laws. He says Jesus Christ has come to change the way we pray and to change our customs."

Point to Stephen.

All those who looked at Stephen saw that his face glowed like an angel's face. The leaders asked, "Are these charges true?" Stephen gave a long, long speech. He told them about God calling Abraham to move to a new land where God would bless him. He told them about Isaac, Jacob, Joseph, and Moses. He said, "I love Moses' words and God's laws. It is your fathers who would not listen to God. Now you won't listen to God either. Your fathers killed God's prophets and you killed God's son, Jesus."

Indicate with a sweeping motion of the hand the large crowd around Stephen.

When the people heard this, they were furious. How could Stephen say such things!

Point to Stephen, and then look up.

Stephen looked up and said, "I see heaven open and Jesus standing at the right hand of God."

Point to the crowd.

At these words, the crowd was even more furious.

Cover your ears.

They covered their ears and yelled with loud voices so they couldn't hear what Stephen said.

Begin moving the figures to the left side of the underlay.

Then they grabbed Stephen and dragged him out of town.

Have the figures reach the left side. Set Stephen by himself. Throw the stones at him.

There the people threw big stones at Stephen. Just before he died, Stephen prayed, "Lord Jesus, let me go to be with you. And please, forgive these people for their sins."

Lay Stephen down on the underlay.

With these words Stephen died.

Pause and reflect on the whole scene.

Begin the wondering time.

I wonder what it was like to tell others about Jesus and have many believe.

I wonder how Stephen felt when he was chosen to help the poor.

I wonder why some people did not like what Stephen said about Jesus.

I wonder how Stephen felt when he was arrested for preaching.

I wonder how Stephen felt when the stones were hitting him.

I wonder how Stephen felt when he prayed and saw Jesus.

I wonder if more people will believe in Jesus after what happened to Stephen.

I wonder if there are people today who are being hurt in some way because they tell others about Jesus. I wonder how they feel.

I wonder if any one of you has told someone about Jesus, and that person laughed at you or was angry.

Return to the worship outline and continue.

46

Paul and Silas in Jail

Scripture source: Acts 16:16–40

Materials:

    Figures of Paul, Silas, girl, and jailer

    Green underlay

    Blue felt (6" x 22")

    Jail background

    Basket to hold figures

Scripture to read: Acts 16:16–19, 22–34

Bible marker: A picture of Paul with his feet in stocks and singing to remind us of the time Paul and Silas were thrown in jail but they rejoiced anyway and the jailer was saved

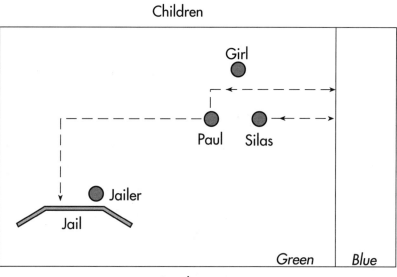

Carefully spread out the green underlay.	Today we are in the Season of Pentecost. It is the time when we learn about more and more people believing in Jesus.
Present Paul.	Paul had come to the city of Philippi to tell others about Jesus. Lydia and her family heard, believed, and were baptized. Paul and his helpers stayed at Lydia's home while they were in Philippi.
Set Paul in the middle of the underlay. Present Silas.	Silas was a missionary who, like Paul, told others about Jesus.
Set Silas next to Paul.	
Add the blue felt along the right edge. Move Paul and Silas until they reach the edge of the felt.	Each day Paul and Silas walked from Lydia's home to the riverside to pray. It was important to talk with God every day. So Paul and Silas prayed every day.
Move them back to the middle of the underlay.	Each day as Paul and Silas went to pray, they were met by
Present the girl.	a slave girl who had an evil spirit living in her. The evil spirit spoke through the girl, telling people what would happen to them in the future. The slave girl's owners made a lot of money from the girl's fortune telling.
Set the girl next to Paul and Silas.	Every time the girl saw Paul and Silas, she would shout, "These men are servants of the Most High God." She did this for many days.
Point to Paul.	Finally one day Paul turned to her and said to the evil spirit, "In the name of Jesus Christ I command you to come out of her!"
Point to the girl.	At that very moment the evil spirit left the girl. Now the girl's owners were angry. They couldn't make money from her anymore.
Remove the girl from the scene. Put her back in the basket.	The girl's owners grabbed Paul and Silas and dragged them to the town officials in the public square. "These Jews are causing trouble," they said. "They are teaching things that are against our law. We can't let them do this."

With a sweeping motion of the hand indicate a large crowd around Paul and Silas.

Soon a large crowd gathered. "Punish them! Punish them!" everyone shouted. So the officials tore the clothes from Paul and Silas. They had them beaten in front of everyone.

Add the jail background to the far left of the underlay.

Then they brought them to jail.

Put Paul and Silas in front of the jail. Add the jailer to the scene.

Here the officials gave them to the jailer who put them way in the inner prison and fastened their feet to blocks of wood.

Point to Paul and Silas.

Their backs were hurt and bleeding, but Paul and Silas were joyful. They were happy because God was with them and they were still alive so they could tell others about Jesus. They were happy because the girl was healed. Jesus was more powerful than the evil spirit.

Pause.

During the night Paul and Silas sang and prayed. They told the other prisoners and the jailer about God's love. The prisoners listened.

Point to the jailer.

The jailer heard the praying and singing. He went to check it out. What was going on? What was the noise? It sounded like singing but the jailer had never heard prisoners sing before. Usually they were angry.

Begin jiggling the background to simulate an earthquake.

As the jailer walked through the prison, he felt the ground shake. The prison was moving! The earthquake was so violent that the locked prison doors flew open and all the chains fell from the prisoners' arms and ankles.

Set the background down. Point to the jailer.

When the jailer saw that all the prison doors were open, he thought that surely all the prisoners had run away. *They must have all escaped,* he thought, *and now I'll be killed in their place.* So he took his sword and got ready to kill himself.

Point to Paul.

Paul quickly shouted, "Don't hurt yourself! We are all here. No one ran away."

Point to the jailer.

The jailer found a light and fell down before Paul and Silas. He was so scared he was shaking all over. "Oh, sirs," he said. "What must I do to be saved?"

Point to Paul and Silas.

"Believe in the Lord Jesus, and you will be saved," replied Paul and Silas.

Move the jailer, Paul, and Silas to the middle of the underlay.

The jailer took Paul and Silas to his own home. He washed their backs where they had been beaten and gave them food to eat.

Point to Paul and Silas.

Paul and Silas told the jailer and his whole family about Jesus.

Point to the jailer and make a circular motion around him to indicate his family.

The jailer and his whole family believed in Jesus. They were baptized. The jailer and his family were filled with joy because now they were Christians.

Pause and reflect on the whole scene.

Begin the wondering time.

I wonder how Paul and Silas felt as they went each day to pray.

Remind the children of the slave girl and what she said.

I wonder why Paul and Silas healed the girl.

I wonder how the slave girl's owners felt when she was healed.

I wonder how it felt to be beaten with rods and thrown into prison.

I wonder why Paul and Silas sang and prayed in prison.

What happened because they sang and prayed?

I wonder how the jailer felt during the earthquake.

I wonder how Paul and Silas felt during the earthquake.

I wonder how the jailer and his family felt at the end of the story.

I wonder who else will believe in Jesus.

Return to the worship outline and continue.

Part Five

Patterns and Instructions

47

Figure Patterns

The figures can be cut out of any one-inch wood or three-fourths-inch plywood. Whatever is available at a reasonable cost is best. White pine is easy to use and looks good when the figures are finished.

Check with local lumber yards for wood. They may also have scrap barrels that you may go through to find wood that is appropriate. Some retailers may be willing to donate scrap pieces if they know you are using them to make Bible figures for church.

Try to find someone from your own church family to cut out the figures. It will save on cost and, more importantly, involve that person in a significant and valuable ministry.

If you cannot find someone, the figures, backgrounds, and other story props are available from YOUNGSTIRS, Steve and Mary DeYoung, 99 West 18th Street, Holland, MI 49423, (616) 396-3445. Write or call for a price list of the figures and backgrounds for the stories in *Leading Children in Worship, Book 2*.

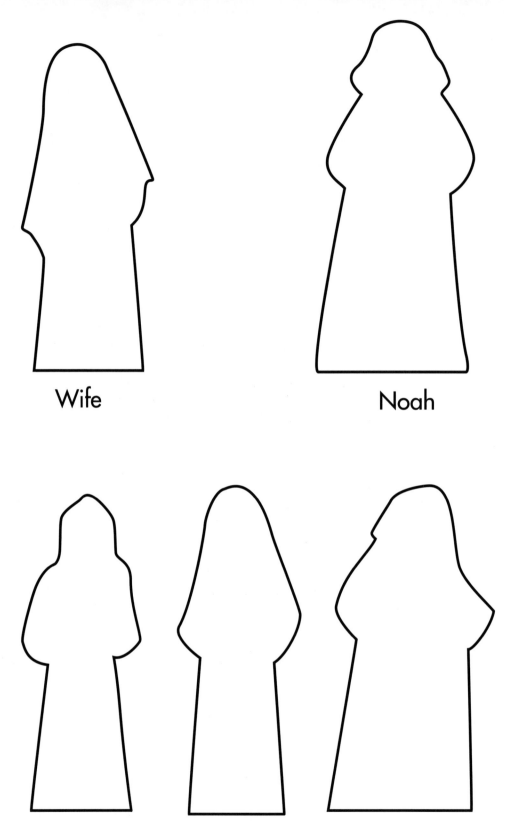

Wife

Noah

Sons' Wives

Noah's sons

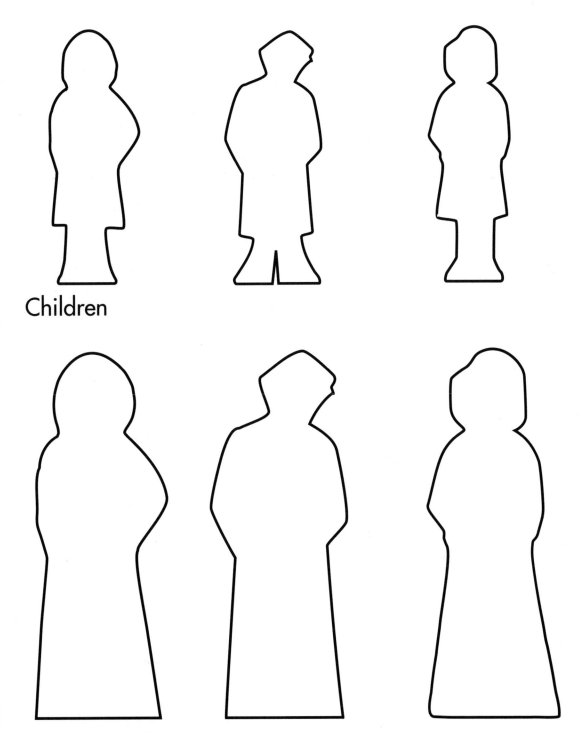

Children

Adults

Bear cut 2

Male lion

Elephant cut 2

Dove

Female lion

Bird cut 2

Pig cut 2

Horse cut 2

glue one to each side
to make the ram

cut 2

cut 2

Ram and Sheep

Bull

cut 2

Giraffe

Cow

cut 2

Camel

cut 2
(1 without horns)

Moose

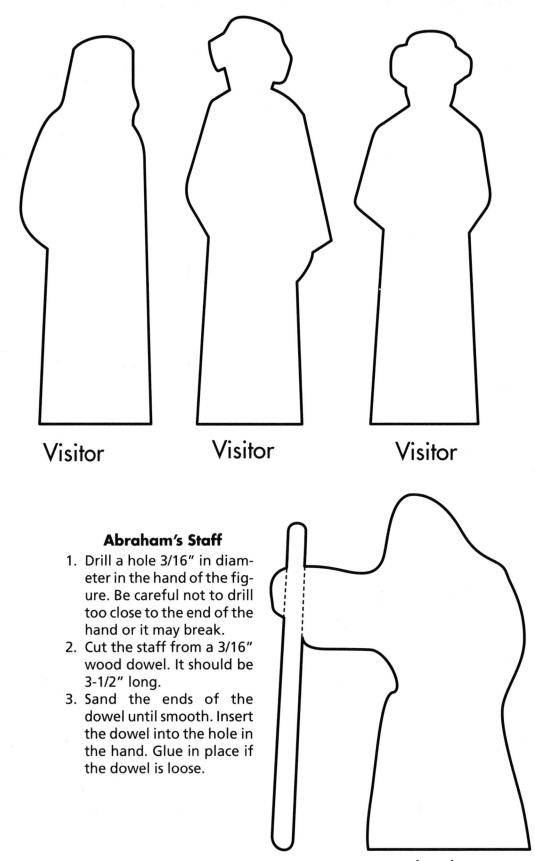

Visitor

Visitor

Visitor

Abraham's Staff

1. Drill a hole 3/16" in diameter in the hand of the figure. Be careful not to drill too close to the end of the hand or it may break.
2. Cut the staff from a 3/16" wood dowel. It should be 3-1/2" long.
3. Sand the ends of the dowel until smooth. Insert the dowel into the hole in the hand. Glue in place if the dowel is loose.

Abraham

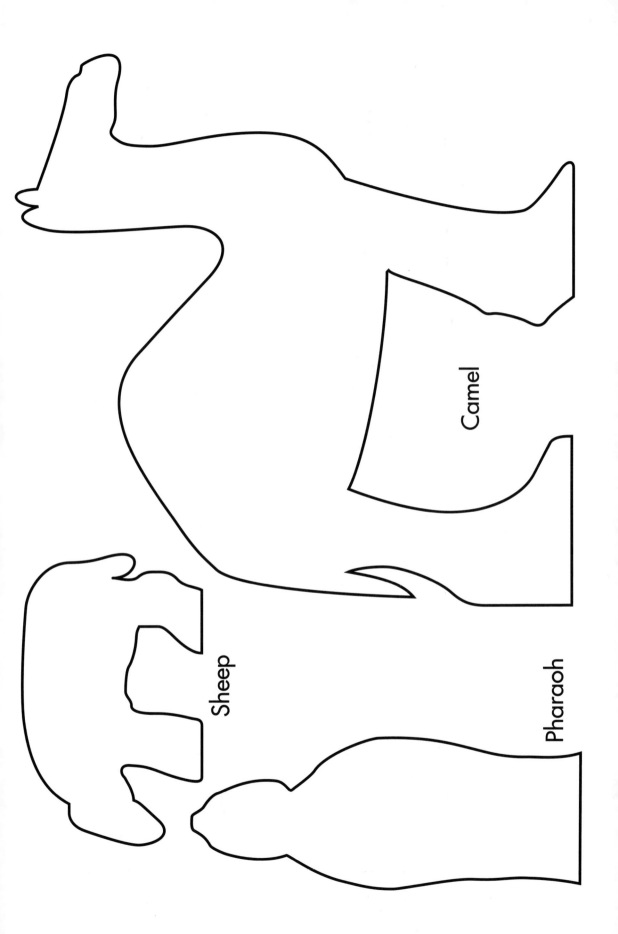

Camel

Sheep

Pharaoh

Men   Choose any one wherever needed.

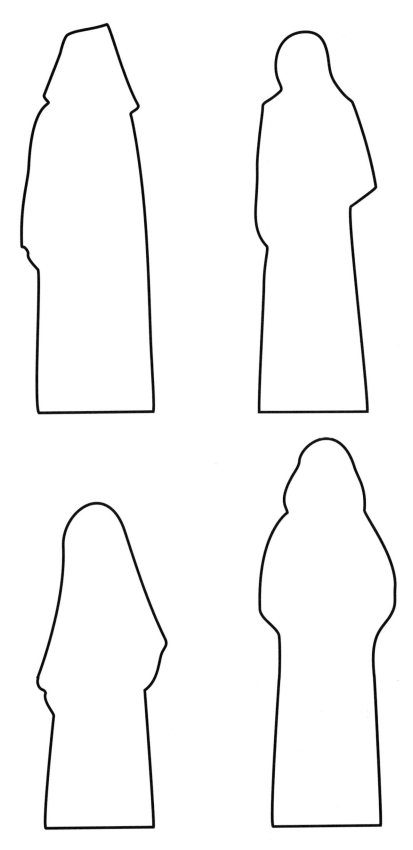

Men

Men

Children

Choose any one for the stories with children.

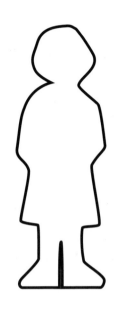
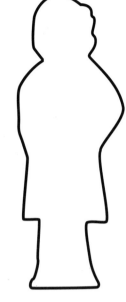

Women

Choose any one wherever needed.

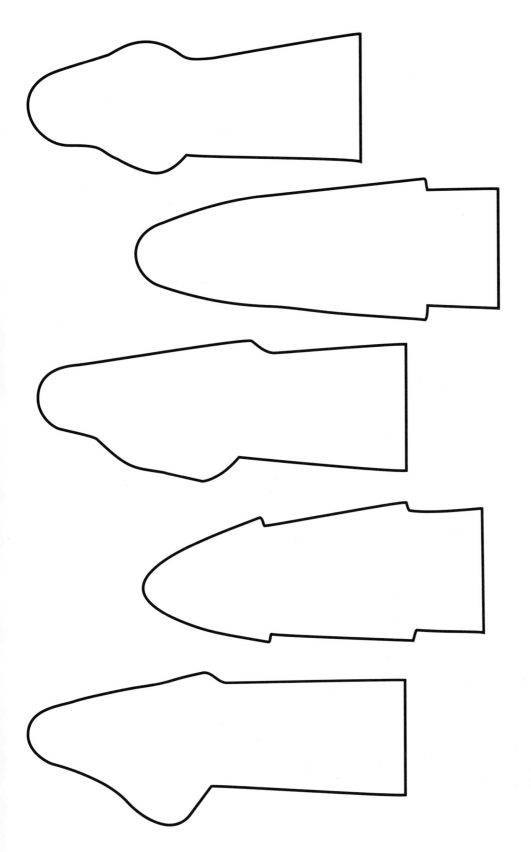

Women

Cut out the figure so he can be moved in and out of the whale.

Jonah and the Whale

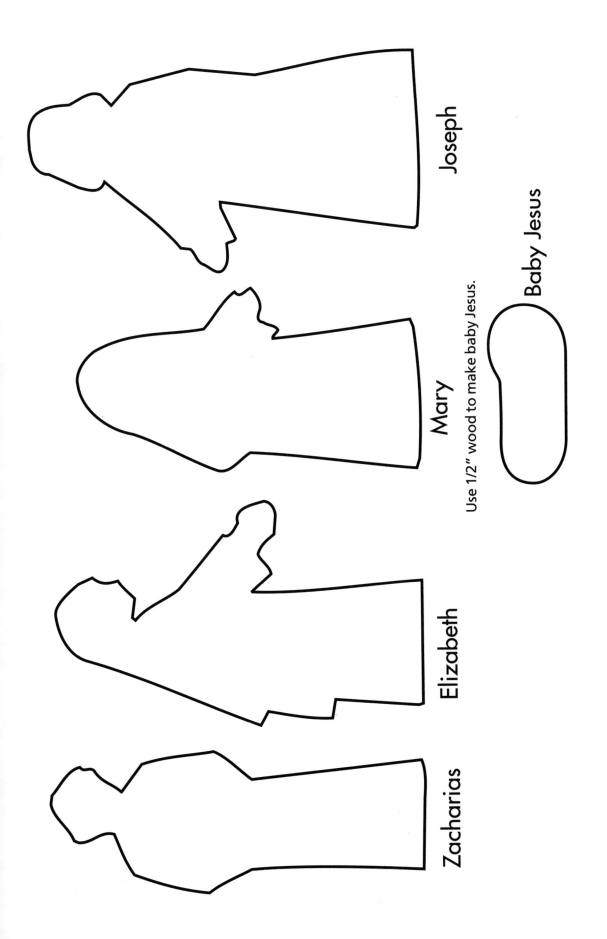

Joseph

Mary

Baby Jesus

Use 1/2" wood to make baby Jesus.

Elizabeth

Zacharias

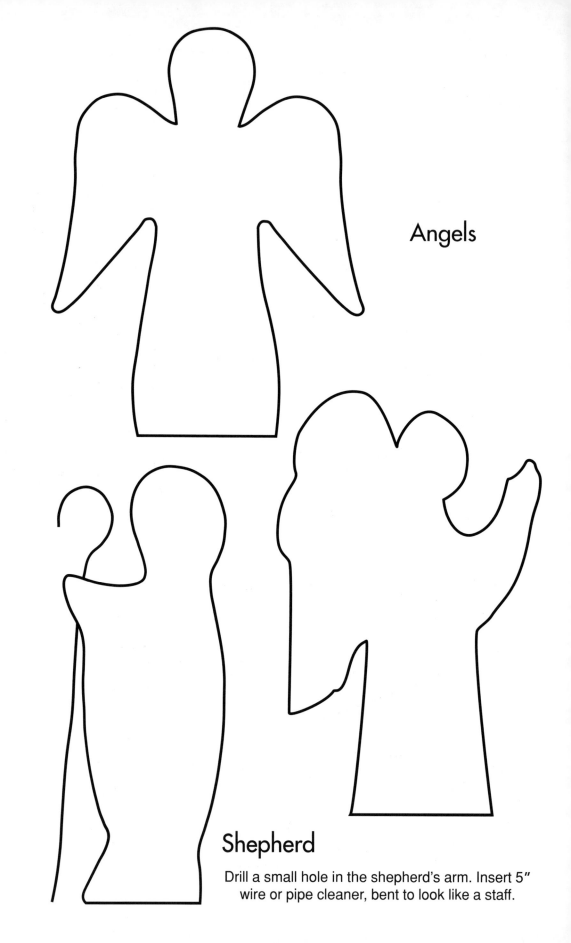

Angels

Shepherd

Drill a small hole in the shepherd's arm. Insert 5″ wire or pipe cleaner, bent to look like a staff.

Jesus

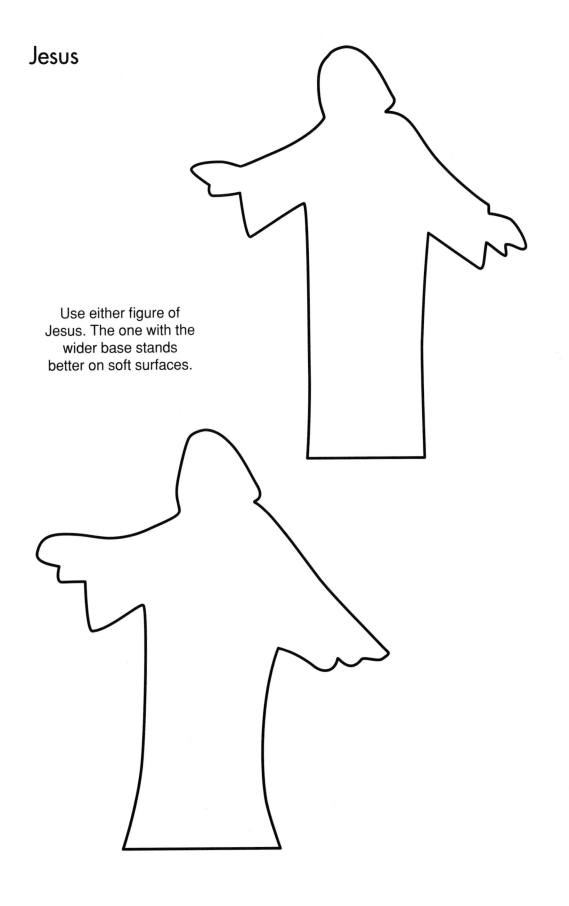

Use either figure of
Jesus. The one with the
wider base stands
better on soft surfaces.

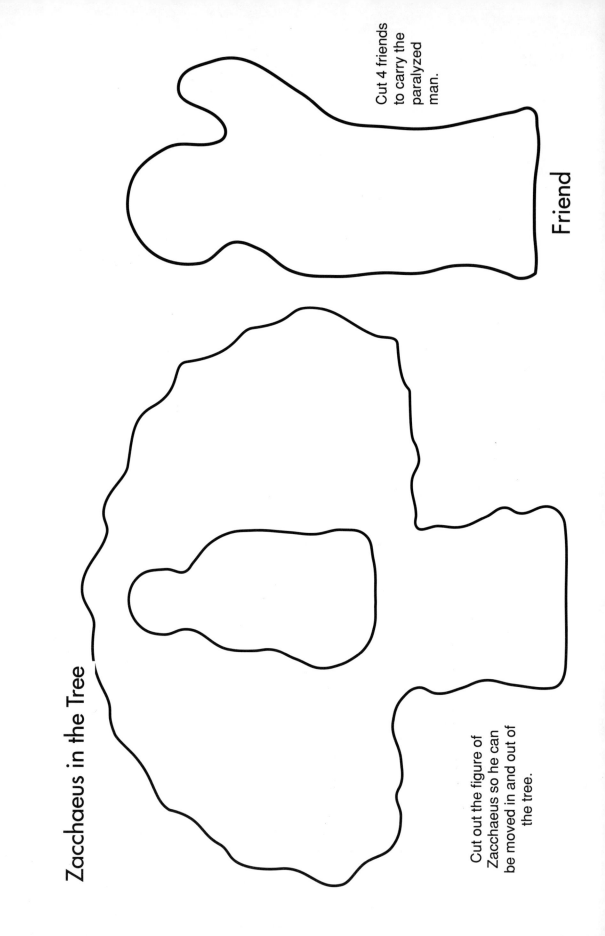

Zacchaeus in the Tree

Friend

Cut 4 friends to carry the paralyzed man.

Cut out the figure of Zacchaeus so he can be moved in and out of the tree.

The Disciples

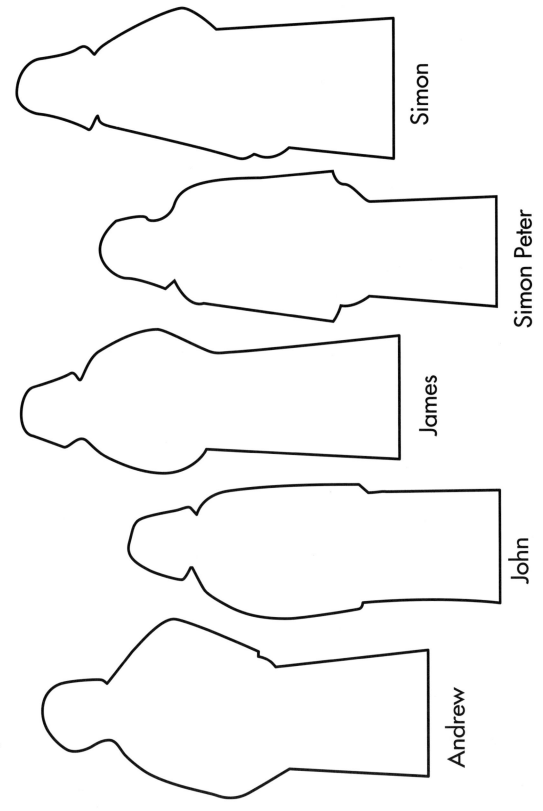

Simon

Simon Peter

James

John

Andrew

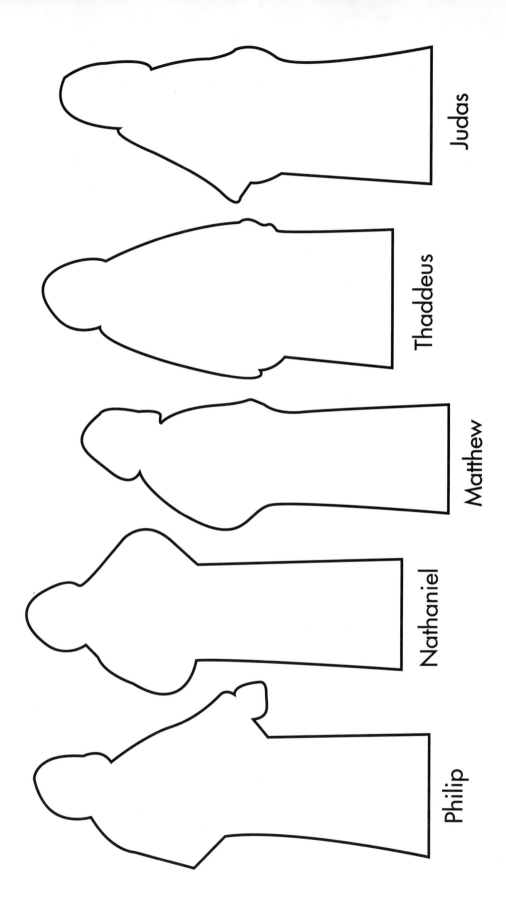

Judas

Thaddeus

Matthew

Nathaniel

Philip

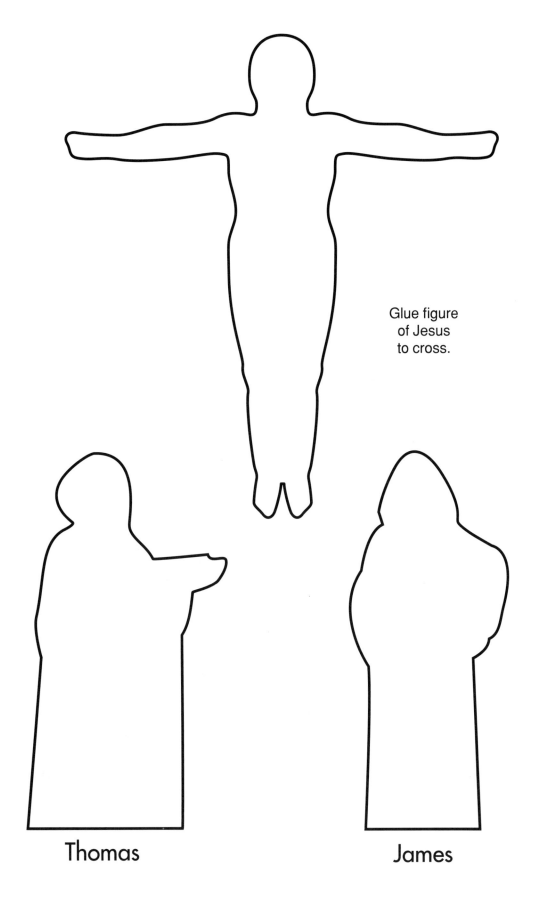

Glue figure
of Jesus
to cross.

Thomas

James

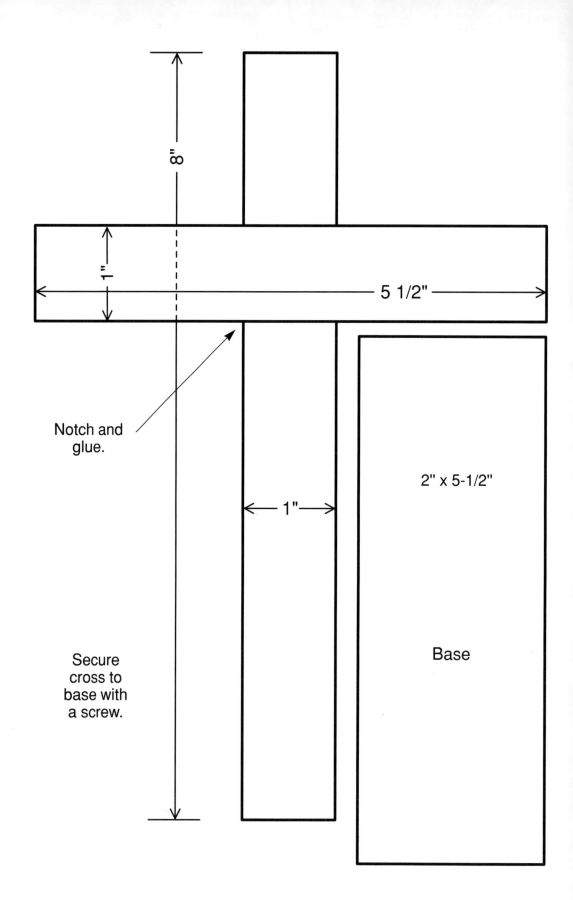

8"

1"

5 1/2"

Notch and
glue.

1"

2" x 5-1/2"

Base

Secure
cross to
base with
a screw.

Jesus on the Donkey

Pastors

Figures from around the World

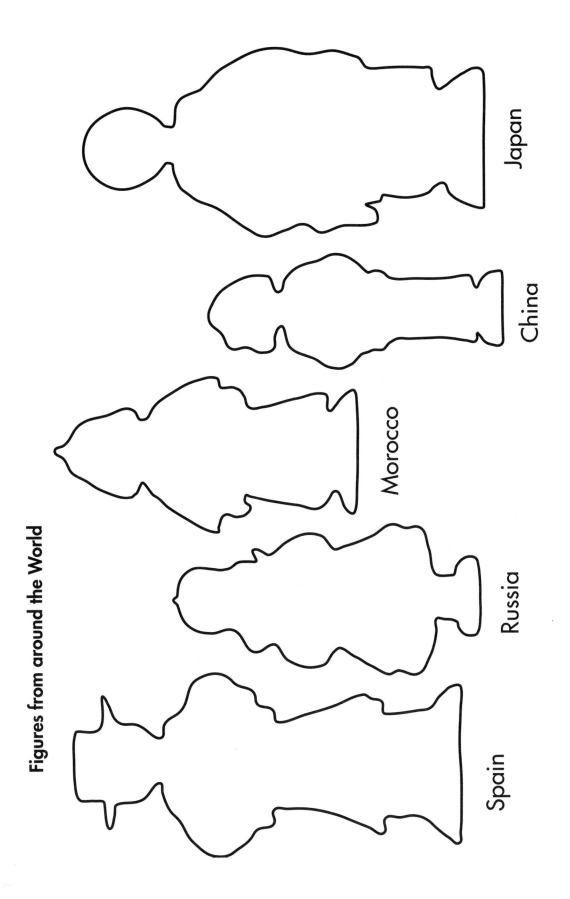

Japan

China

Morocco

Russia

Spain

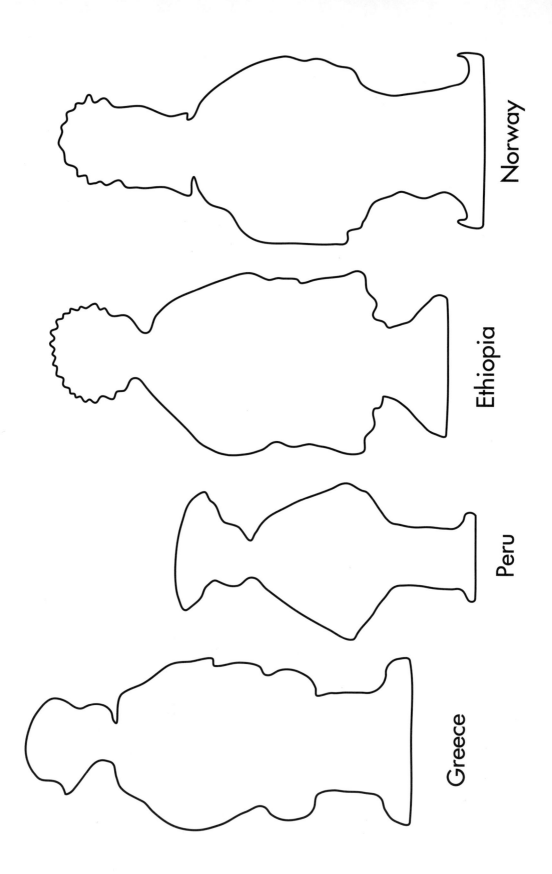

Norway

Ethiopia

Peru

Greece

Netherlands

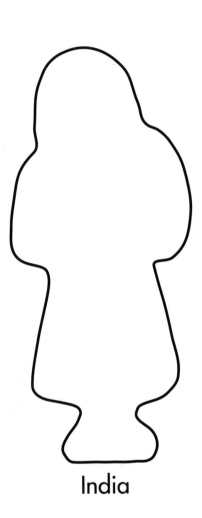

India

48

Underlays

To make an underlay, cut one yard of 44″-wide cotton-blend material in half lengthwise. Hem the three raw edges leaving the selvage edge as is. One yard will make two underlays of 22″ x 36″ each.

For the stories in this book you will need:

    17 green underlays
    2 blue underlays
    3 sand-colored underlays
    3 white underlays
    2 purple underlays

It is best to have a separate underlay to be stored with each story.

An additional green underlay of 44″ x 36″ is used for "The Ten Plagues" story. Two purple felt underlays of 18″ x 72″ are used for the Lent series and a piece of white felt 9″ x 72″ is used as an underlay for "The Lord's Prayer" story. If only single-width felt is available, sew two pieces of the correct width together to get the correct length.

49

Backgrounds

Use 1/4″ or 1/8″ plywood for the backgrounds. The center piece is 8-1/2″ x 12″ and the two side pieces are 8-1/2″ x 6″ (see diagram on next page). Hinge the pieces together with strapping tape or material glued to the back. The backgrounds will stand up for the stories and fold up for storage.

Cut windows, doors, and whatever else is needed out of pieces of material and glue these on to the backgrounds, or paint the scene on the background.

The backgrounds, when folded, are used as trays, holding the underlays and baskets of materials both when bringing the stories to the worship center and when storing the stories on the shelves.

The backgrounds needed for the stories in this book are listed below:

- "God Destroys Sodom"—the inside of a house
  Use a single board of 8-1/2″ x 12″ for the outside of a city with a gate. It sits in front of the house to make the city.
- "Jonah"—city streets of Nineveh
- "Mary Visits Elizabeth"—the inside of a house on both sides
- "Jesus' First Miracle"—the inside of a house
- "Jesus Heals Peter's Mother-in-Law"—a house on one side and a synagogue on the other side
- "Jesus Heals a Paralytic"—the inside of a house
  Use a single board of 8-1/2″ x 12″ for the outside of a house. It sits in front of the inside of the house to make a rectangle so the boards for the roof can be put on top.

- "Mary and Martha"—the inside of a house
- "Zacchaeus"—the city of Jericho
- "Jesus Prays"—a garden
- "We Talk with God at Home"—the inside of a house
- "Paul and Silas in Jail"—the inside of a jail

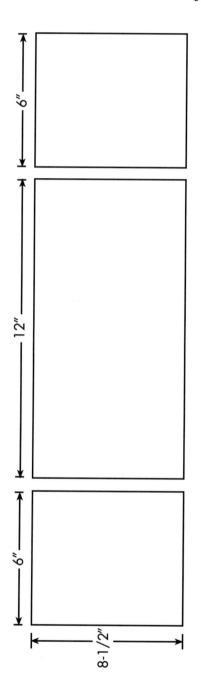

50

Other Props
and Story Materials

Baskets and trays used to hold materials can be purchased, made, or donated. Oval baskets can be used as boats in the stories that need a boat: "Jonah," "Jesus Walks on Water," and "We Talk with God Everywhere." Spray paint old or used trays to make them look new. Plastic dishpans are a good size for the Lent series.

Use flat pieces of felt in appropriate colors for roads, lakes, leaves, branches, and for the figures and other items needed in the Gold Box stories.

"Noah Loves God"

Tent—Use a 12″ x 9″ piece of plywood for the base. Glue two 4-1/2″ pieces of 1/8″ dowel on the board 6-1/2″ apart. Stretch a heavy string, 18-1/2″ long across the dowels. Glue the string to the dowels. There should be about 6″ free at each end. Secure both ends of the string to the base with thumb tacks and glue. Stretch a 6-1/2″ x 12″ piece of leather or denim over the string and secure to the base on both sides with thumb tacks and glue.

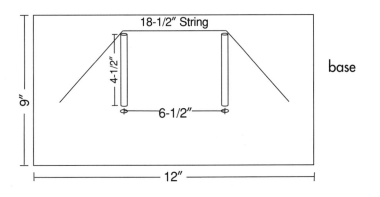

"Noah Obeys God"

Ark
Materials
    1/2" clear plywood or white pine
    5/8" clear plywood or white pine
    1/4" clear plywood or white pine
(See diagram on pages 239–40.)

1. Using the pattern, cut two end pieces from 1/2" plywood or white pine.
2. Cut two 3-1/2" x 14" side pieces from 1/2" plywood or white pine.
3. Cut one 6" x 18" bottom piece from 5/8" plywood or white pine.
4. Cut two 4" x 16" roof pieces from 1/2" plywood or white pine.
5. Cut two 1/2" x 3/4" x 14" spacer pieces from 1/2" plywood or white pine. (The spacers go on the bottom of the ark.)
6. Cut one 1/2" x 1/2" x 13-7/8" brace for the removable roof board.
7. Glue and nail the two spacer pieces to the bottom piece of the ark, as shown in diagram.
8. Glue and nail the two side pieces and two end pieces together making a rectangular box.
9. Glue and nail the rectangular box to the bottom piece, leaving 1-1/2" at each end of the bottom board, as shown.
10. Glue the 1/2" x 1/2" x 13-7/8" brace to one roof board, as shown in the diagram.
11. Glue and nail the other roof board to the top of the ark.
12. Fit the roof board with brace onto the other side of roof. Be sure the brace is propped against the side of the ark, as shown in diagram. Do not nail in place so that this roof board can be removed.
13. Leave the ark unfinished or paint it the color of your choice.

"Noah Thanks God"

Rainbow sun-catchers—Stores that sell glass or plastic sun-catchers to hang in windows will usually have a rainbow. Use one in this story.

"God Destroys Sodom"

Flames—Use a piece of 8-1/2" x 12" orange felt. Cut jagged flame shapes along its length. Glue a piece of Velcro to the back. Glue the corresponding piece of Velcro to the top of the city background.

"Isaac and Rebekah"

Well—Cut a 3" x 10" piece of cardboard. Draw stone shapes on the outside with a marker. Tape short ends together to make a tube shape.

Jar—Use pattern to cut from wood. Spray paint brown.

Noah's Ark

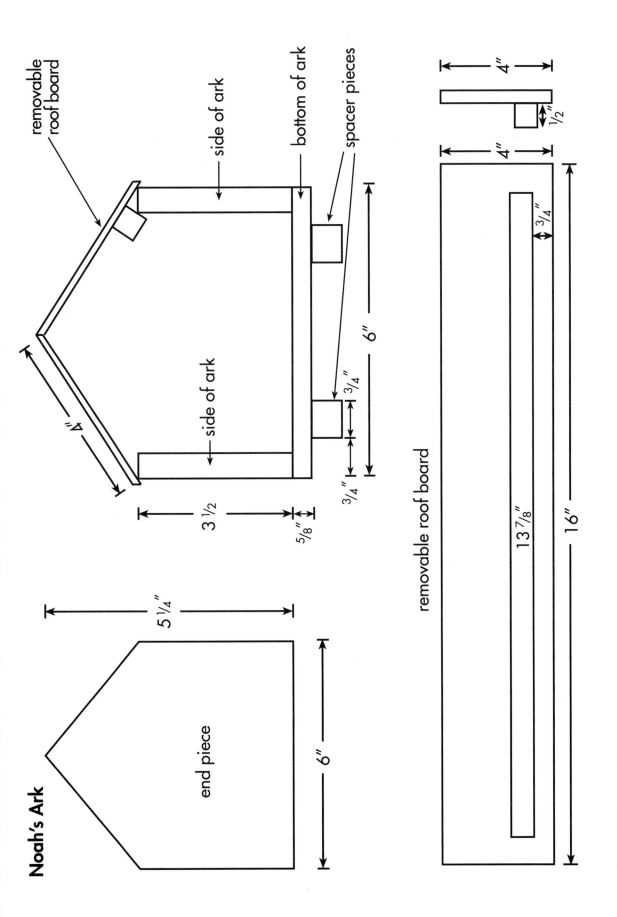

removable roof board

side of ark

bottom of ark

spacer pieces

side of ark

4"

3 ½

5/8"

3/4"

3/4"

6"

5 ¼"

end piece

6"

removable roof board

4"

½"

4"

3/4"

13 7/8"

16"

Side View of Ark

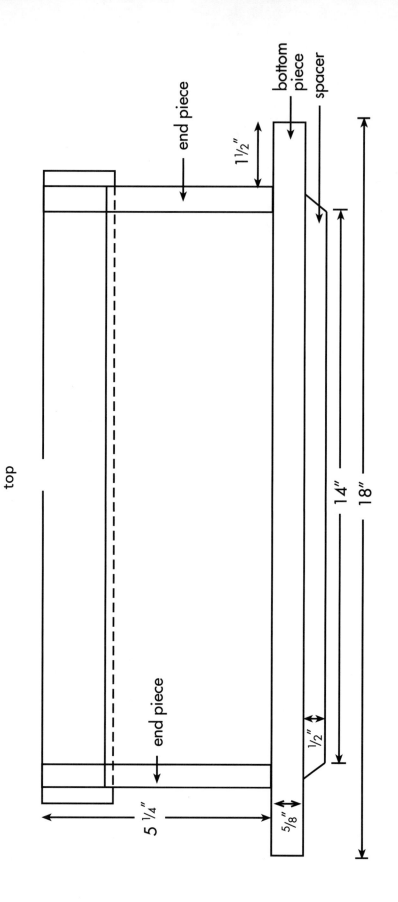

"Esau and Jacob"

Tent—See directions under "Noah Loves God."
Stones—Use several stones to pile on each other for an altar.

"Jacob's Dream"

Stairs—Use four craft sticks. Cut two in half and glue the halves to the two other sticks to make stairs.
Angels—Find a picture of a group of angels, cover with clear Con-Tact paper, and cut out.
Veil—Use a small piece of white material.
Well—See directions under "Isaac and Rebekah."
Stones—Use one stone that can stand on end for Jacob's dream and several others to make an altar.

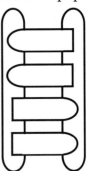

"Burning Bush"

Bush—Use a picture of a bush in flames, cut out, and glue to a piece of wood cut in the same shape as the bush.
Well—See directions under "Isaac and Rebekah."
Shepherd's staff—Use a reed or a 6″ pipe cleaner bent to look like a staff.

"Manna and Water"

Rock—Use a fist-sized rock with a piece of blue felt 1-1/2″ x 3″ glued to it. Roll the felt up to the rock and unroll it in the story.

"The Twelve Spies"

Cloud/fire—Color and cut out picture of a cloud and of fire. Glue to opposite sides of a piece of wood.

"Christmas"

Manger—The manger can be a 3″ piece of 1-3/4″ cove molding. Glue ends on it if you like or use as is.
Stable—Any stable that will hold the wooden figures is fine, or make one using the following pattern.
Materials
    1/2″ plywood
    3/16″ plywood
(See diagram on page 243.)

1. Using the pattern, cut two side pieces from 1/2″ plywood.
2. Cut a 6″ x 12″ bottom piece from 3/16″ plywood. Cut a 7″ x 12″ roof piece from 3/16″ plywood. Cut a 1-1/2″ x 10″ back piece from 3/16″ plywood.
3. Glue and nail the back piece to the two side pieces.

4. Glue and nail the bottom piece to the two side pieces with the bottom board extending 1″ from each side.
5. Glue and nail the roof board to the top of the two side pieces with the roof board extending 1″ from each side.
6. Leave the stable unfinished or paint it the color of your choice.

"Jesus' First Miracle"

Jars—See directions under "Isaac and Rebekah."
Small basin—Use a miniature or make one of dough and let dry.
Plates and cups—Use miniatures or make of dough, let dry, and spray paint.
Small table—See directions below.
Table
(See diagram on page 245.)
Materials
 1/2″ clear white pine or plywood for table top
 3/4″ clear white pine or plywood for the legs

For the large table:

1. Cut a 8″ x 3″ table top.
2. Using the pattern, cut two legs.
3. Glue legs to table top 1″ from each end.

For the small table:

1. Cut a 5″ x 3″ table top.
2. Cut two legs, following the pattern for the large table.
3. Glue legs to table top 3/4″ from each end.

"Jesus Heals Peter's Mother-in-Law"

Mat—Use a 2″ x 5″ piece of material.

"Jesus Heals a Paralytic"

Mat—Use a 4″ x 5″ piece of material. Sew narrow hems along the long edges for two 6″ dowels to slide through.
Platform—Use two pieces of 1/4″ wood. Bottom layer: 7″ x 8″. Top layer: Same size with 1-1/2″ x 3″ cut out of the corners as places for the four friends to stand. Glue the pieces of wood together.

"Lost Coin"

Gold box—Use a shoe box with lid, spray painted gold.
Coins—Make ten coins of paper, poster board, or cardboard. Spray paint silver and cover with clear Con-Tact paper or cover with foil. Silver plugs from electrical boxes can also be used.

Stable

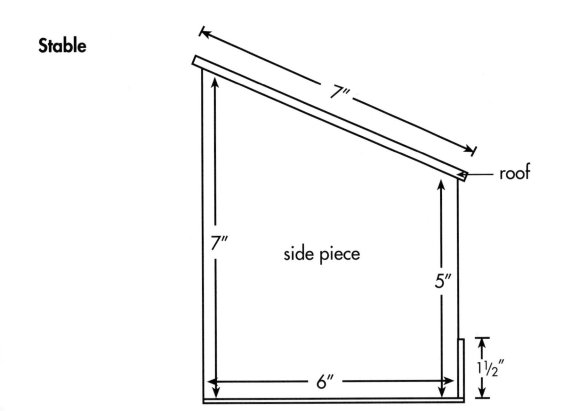

7"

roof

7"

side piece

5"

6"

1½"

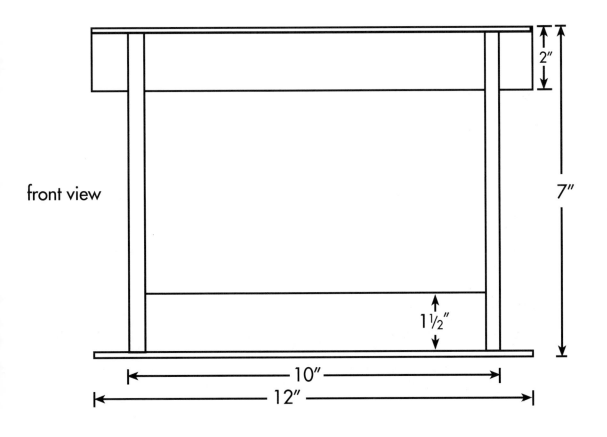

front view

2"

7"

1½"

10"

12"

Lent Series

Purple basket—Use any purple container measuring about 12″ x 14″. Use two-pound cheese boxes to set the figures in a row upright in the basket or container.

Tomb—Use half of a two-pound cheese box as a frame and shape a rounded tomb with patching plaster. Leave an opening the size of a frozen-juice-can lid and large enough to slide Lazarus through. Build the tomb on a 6″ x 9″ board (or a board that fits into the purple container). Cutting off one corner of the board makes it easier to lift out of the container. For the door of the tomb, cover a frozen-juice-can lid with patching plaster.

"Mary and Martha"

Plates and dishes—Use miniatures or doll house dishes appropriate to New Testament times.

Small table—See directions under "Jesus' First Miracle."

"Transfiguration"

Mountain—Make one of papier-mâché or foam. Spray paint. Make it high enough to look like a mountain yet small enough to fit into the purple container with all the other materials.

"Cleansing the Temple"

Coins—See directions under "Lost Coin."
Coats—Use 3″ x 4″ pieces of material with various patterns.
Small tables—See directions under "Jesus' First Miracle."

"Widow's Mite"

Offering box—Use a small box with a cover. Punch a hole in the cover. Form a 2-1/2″ circle of poster board, cut out a wedge large enough to form a cone by overlapping the edges. Glue edges and push the small end into the hole in the box. Spray paint gold.

"Washing the Disciples' Feet"

Basin—Use a miniature bowl or make one of dough, let dry, and spray paint.
Towel—Use a 3″ square of terry cloth.
Large table—See directions under "Jesus' First Miracle."

Large Table

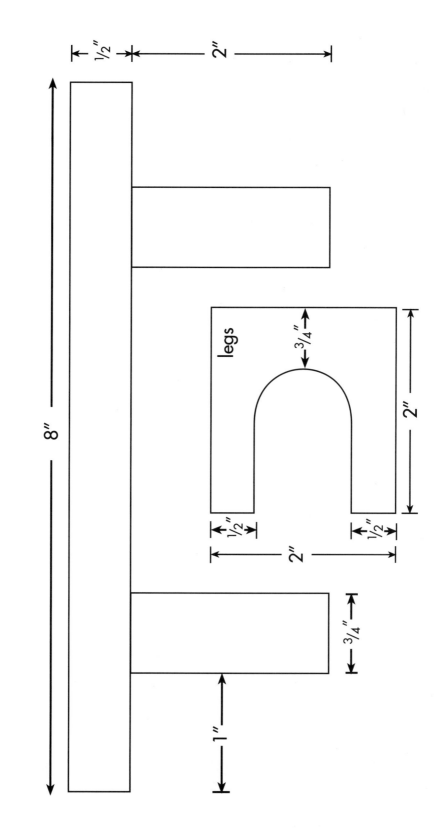

"We Talk with God in Prayer"

Mountain—See directions under "Transfiguration." This one can be larger with steeper sides.

"We Talk with God at Home"

Table—See directions under "Jesus' First Miracle." Make the small table. (See diagram on page 245.)

Bed

Materials

3/4″ clear white pine or plywood

1. Using the patterns below, cut the head and foot pieces.
2. Cut a 3″ x 3-1/2″ center piece.
3. Fasten the head and foot pieces to the center piece using carpenter's glue and 1″ brads.

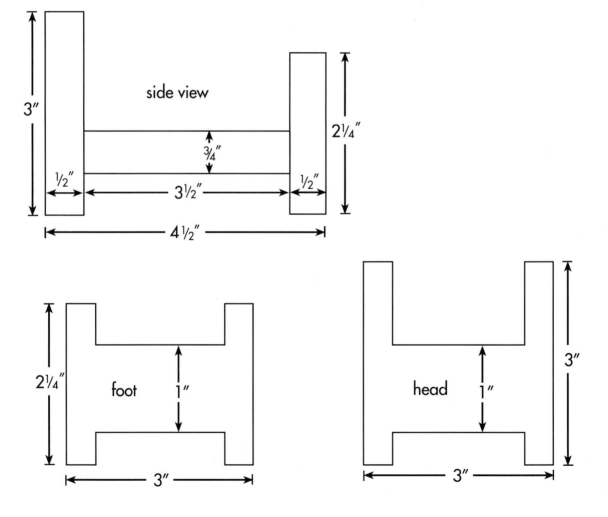

"We Talk with God at Church"

Temple

Materials

Any 3/4″ lumber pieces for the base, top, and bottom

3/4″ dowel for the pillars

(See diagram below, shown 1/2 actual size.)

1. Cut one 6″ x 10″ base board.
2. Cut two 4″ x 8″ boards for the top and bottom of the temple.
3. Cut four pillars 3-1/2″ long from the dowel.
4. Place the pillars 1/8″ in from the sides of the top and bottom and fasten with a 1-1/4″ brad and carpenter's glue.
5. When the glue is dry, glue the top part to the base leaving a 1″ step all the way around the temple.
6. Spray with gold paint for a fine finish.

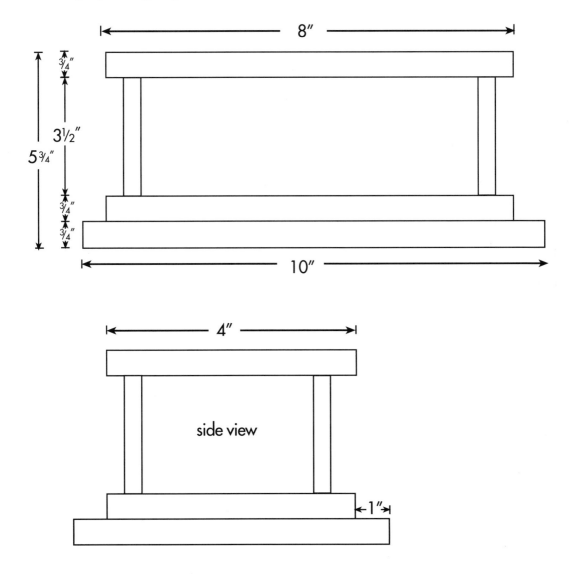

side view

Scroll—Use an 8″ piece of 1/4″ dowel. Cut into two 4″ pieces. Glue ends of a 3-1/2″ x 10″ piece of paper to the dowels. Let dry. Write Psalm 122:1b on the paper. Roll up from both ends and tie with yarn.

Cars—Use small wooden blocks with holes drilled in the tops that the people will fit into. Spray paint in a variety of colors.

People—Craft stores carry small wooden figures that can be used as people, or make them by cutting off the tops of push-type clothespins. Spray paint in a variety of colors.

"Jesus' Example of Prayer"

Mountain—See directions under "Transfiguration."

Plate and chalice—Use miniatures or make of dough, let dry, and spray paint.

Small table—See directions under "Jesus' First Miracle."

Part
Six

Leader Resources

51

Guidelines for Leaders and Helpers

I. Preparing the Leaders
   A. Ask for God's blessing and guidance during the worship time.
   B. Spend some time being quiet, as the children are asked to do, and focus on worshiping God.
   C. Keep conversation with the other leaders and helpers to a minimum, only as it relates to preparing for worship. If administrative details need to be discussed, save them for after the worship service.

II. Preparing the Children
   A. Greet each child warmly, by using his/her name, and when possible, an appropriate touch.
   B. Focus your total attention on the children and ways in which you can help them prepare for worship.
      1. Remember: The children will often follow your example, so speak speak softly, move slowly, focus on preparing for worship.
      2. Be down on the floor with them, available to watch, listen, and guide.

III. Circle Time—Role of the Helpers
   A. Goal: to help the children remain centered on the presentation.
      1. Children should sit at their place in circle, with their hands and feet quiet and crossed.
      2. Allow only that conversation that relates to presentation—this needs some leeway, for you cannot know exactly what the Spirit may bring to mind and heart.
      3. Keep distractions to a minimum.
      4. Discipline
         a. First offense: Child should be given a reminder (warning) that what he/she is doing is not acceptable (i.e., "Please hug your hands or your knees").
         b. Second offense: Child is given the choice to ready himself/herself or go to the "get ready" chair (i.e., "You need to hug your knees or go to the 'get ready' chair until you are ready").
         c. Third offense: Child is removed from the circle to the "get ready" chair, outside the worship circle.
      5. Circle helpers should handle as much of the correction as possible so the leader can remain centered on story material and avoid unnecessary interruptions of the presentation.

IV. Work Time
   A. Goal: providing an environment conducive to the child's being able to respond to God's story.
      1. Help children respect others' space, materials, and response time.
      2. Correct children who walk on others' material and/or carpet pieces, are talking to others, or are creating any other type of disruption.
   B. Helpers need to show this same respect.
      1. Do not interrupt children. They can and do learn by their own mistakes and discoveries. Therefore, step back and give way to that beautiful expression a child experiences as he/she responds to the workings of the Spirit.
      Exception: If the children misuse the materials, interrupt them and remind them of the correct way to use the materials.
 V. Regathering for Circle Time
   A. Goal: to help the child make the transition from individual to corporate worship.
      1. Guide and direct children only as necessary.
      2. After work materials have been put away, guide each child back to the circle for sitting and redirection.
VI. Dismissal
   A. Goal: to send the children out in an orderly and positive fashion, affirming each child with a personal good word and dismissing him/her with a blessing.

52

Bible Markers and Take-Home Papers

Bible Markers

Bible markers can be made to accompany each story. Each is made of a 3″ x 5″ piece of paper. (If you use the liturgical colors, the Bible markers can be made of the appropriate colors.) To illustrate the day's story, use pictures you have on hand, stickers, or pictures that the children draw. Your bookstore may have resources containing art that may be reproduced for your local church use. Be sure to check that permission for copying is given on the copyright page.

Each marker should include the following: an appropriate picture, the title of the story, and the "Scripture to read" passage.

For older children, provide a Bible and Bible marker for each child. During the "Closing Circle," the children can find the passage for the day and read it in unison (or the child helper could read the Scripture passage while the other children follow along). This helps the children become better acquainted with the Bible.

Take-Home Papers

Take-home papers can be made to accompany each story. Each is made of an 8-1/2″ x 11″ piece of paper folded in half. On the front cover is the title of the story and the Scripture references. Inside are the words of the Bible story. Sometimes the story needs to be shortened so that it will fit. Also included are as many of the wondering thoughts as space will allow. On the back of the paper is a picture similar to the Bible marker picture.

Take-home papers are given to the children as they leave the worship center. The papers help the children and parents reread the day's Bible story and talk over the story together. We also put a paper in the cubbyhole of the child who is absent so he or she has an opportunity to read the story.

Take-home papers are especially useful if the worship center approach is used during the Sunday school hour when it is customary to send papers home with the children.

Sample Parent Letters

Please feel free to use and adapt these letters and take-home papers to fit your own specific situation. For the orientation lessons, the letter is printed on the inside of a 8-1/2″ x 11″ piece of paper that is folded in half.

Week One of the Children-in-Worship Ministry

The front of the take-home paper says: "Getting Ready to Worship God, Lesson 1." The back has a picture of Jesus blessing the children. It's best to wait until the children and leaders have settled into a routine before inviting parents and others to join them.

Dear Parents:

Your child is beginning an exciting time to be with God, to experience his presence, to hear God's stories, and to listen to God.

For the next three weeks your child will be learning how to get ready to be with God in this special children-in-worship setting.

It is an exciting way for the children to learn their Bible stories because the stories are told using visuals, so the children not only hear the story but also see it and later can use the materials to work with the story themselves.

A number of other important things are learned, too. The children learn to walk and talk quietly, to take care of their things (everything they work with they put back in its proper place), and that this is a holy place where God is. They learn that God loves them, cares for them, and will always be with them just as he loved and cared for Noah, Abraham, Moses, the lost sheep in the Good Shepherd story, blind Bartimaeus, and Zacchaeus.

All of this is done in the worship model and format. Our hour is spent in the same way that the children experience it in the worship service in the sanctuary. The leader and children approach God in reverence, hear his Word, respond in praise, and go forth in peace and love to serve in God's name.

During the Approach to God time, the children learn songs of praise, calls to worship, and the Lord's Prayer. They learn to quiet themselves and prepare to listen to God's Word.

The children both hear and see the stories of God as wooden figures and felt pieces are used to enhance their presentation.

Each story is followed by a wondering time—a time to help the children and leader together to get at the meaning and importance of the Bible story.

After the Word, the children begin a time of working with God's stories. Because children do not easily verbalize their reactions and responses, a variety of art materials is provided with which they can express themselves. They are also free to work with any of the stories that have been previously presented because all of the stories are put on the shelves for the children to use freely.

The stories are shelved sequentially, so the children learn the flow of the Bible; the Old Testament stories are followed by Advent, the nativity, Epiphany, Lent,

Easter, and Pentecost. By the end of the year the children are literally surrounded by God's stories.

Before leaving, the children gather in a closing circle. The Bible is read, emphasizing for the children that the story they heard came from Scripture, prayers are offered, and a "feast" is celebrated. This "feast" is just a snack but it models and helps the children understand the Lord's Supper.

To conclude their worship, the children come individually to the leader for the benediction, a parting blessing: "The love of God be with you. Shalom."

Week Two of the Children-in-Worship Ministry

The front of the take-home paper says: "Getting Ready to Worship God, Lesson 2." The back says: "Worship" written in large, open letters so they can be colored.

Dear Parents:

The children have been learning that the Worship Center is a very special place to be with God. Because it is so special, they have been learning how to get ready to be with God. They learn to walk slowly, to sit on the tape on the floor, and to cross their legs and hug their hands or knees.

They also learn to speak with a soft voice so as not to disturb anyone talking with God. There are different ways to talk with God. When we are with God, sometimes we are so happy that we just have to tell him. So we can sing our thanks. Another way we talk with God is through artwork. We can draw our thanks to God using crayons, markers, chalk, and paper.

The children learn how to take art supplies from the shelves and how to put everything back in its appropriate place. We have a special place to put our work, to keep it safe until it is time to bring the work home.

When worktime is finished, it is time to gather again in the circle to read the Bible and celebrate with a "feast." The children know worktime is finished when a small bell is rung. When they hear the bell, they carefully put away all their materials. The Worship Center belongs to them and they are responsible for keeping it tidy and neat.

To get ready for the Bible reading and for the "feast," everyone again sits on the tape. The story of the day is always read from the Bible and a marker put in that place so we can go back to re-read the story from the Bible.

When we have a "feast," napkins are spread on the floor and a simple snack of crackers and juice or something similar is shared. During this time the children learn to say "thank you" prayers to God.

When our time together is over, all the children come to the leader for a personal Benediction. Each child is also given an encouraging word about what he/she did during our time together.

The children-in-worship format is a rich and deep ministry that helps the children learn their Bible stories very well and worship God reverently.

Week Three of the Children-in-Worship Ministry

The front of the take-home paper says: "Getting Ready to Worship God, Lesson 3." The back says: "Be still . . . I am God" written in dotted letters so the children can trace over them.

Dear Parents:

Today was our last "getting ready" lesson. Together we reviewed that the Worship Center is a very special place to be with God, to talk with God, to listen to God, and to hear the stories of God.

We reviewed how to walk slowly, to speak softly so as not to disturb someone else who may be talking with God, and to sit on the tape and cross our legs and hug our hands or our knees.

We learned to greet each other by saying, "The Lord be with you. And also with you."

We reviewed how to get our art materials and how to put everything away to keep our Worship Center tidy and neat. We reviewed that when the small bell in the room is rung, we clean up our work area. We put our artwork in a special place either to take home or to keep to finish next week.

The children have learned that one of the ways to come close to God is by becoming very quiet and listening. Quietness comes from within; they can become quiet all by themselves. They also learned a new song to help them become quiet, "Be Still and Know that I Am God." They learned how to make their bodies very still to help them get quiet so they can listen to God and his stories.

We reviewed how to get ready to hear the Bible read and how to find the stories in the Bible. We reviewed how to get ready for the feast.

Finally, we reviewed that before we leave, we each receive an individual blessing.

Next week we will begin hearing Bible stories. A paper will come home each week with the words of the story and some thoughts for you as parents to talk over with your child.

After we have settled into our routine, please feel free to come and visit us. We encourage and welcome parents to come anytime to join us in this exciting time in God's presence.

Use the following letter for the older children:

Dear Parents:

We begin a new year of Sunday School today. Our basis is worshiping God and our outline each week follows the worship outline: Drawing Near to God, Listening to God's Word, Responding to God's Word, and then receiving a Benediction.

During the Drawing Near to God time, we sing, pray, and quiet ourselves so we can listen to God. During the Listening to God's Word time, the children hear a story from the Bible, usually accompanied by wooden figures and other story props. After the story, the children choose how they want to work with God's stories. There are puzzles, books, pictures to color, and many other activities for the children to choose from. We always gather together again and find where in the Bible our story of the day was taken from. The older children read the passage together and then the child helper for the day says a prayer. During the Responding to God's Word time, we sometimes celebrate a feast which helps the children understand the Lord's Supper. The leader always closes with a Benediction. The children also give the closing blessing, so they learn that they can bless and encourage each other.

The children-in-worship ministry is an exciting way to be in the presence of God as adults and children. Please take the time to come and join us. We welcome parents, grandparents, and all others anytime.

Each week a take-home paper is given to the children. It would really reinforce the day's Bible story if you could take a few minutes to read the paper and go over the wondering thoughts with your child. We also encourage you to take time every day to read the Bible or Bible stories and pray. This will enhance your child's spiritual growth and walk with the Lord.

I have enclosed a list of the Bible stories we will hear this year so you know what we will be studying. Also attached is the list of Bible verses we will be learning each month. We say them several times each Sunday during the month but help in learning them is greatly appreciated.

If at any time you have any questions or concerns, please feel free to call or drop by for a visit.

Thank you for allowing me the privilege of worshiping each week with your child. God's presence is so very real in our Worship Center. May God richly bless you as you guide your family in his way.

53

Bible Verses to Memorize

T he children learn one Bible verse a month. Repeat it before the prayer and story time, after the wondering time, or during the Bible reading time.

Year One

September: Let us go to the house of the Lord. Psalm 122:1
October: Jesus said, "I am the light of the world." John 8:12
November: It is good to praise the Lord. Psalm 92:1
December: Jesus was born in Bethlehem. Matthew 2:1.
January: Be kind . . . to one another. Ephesians 4:32
February: Let us love one another. 1 John 4:7
March: [God] cares for you. 1 Peter 5:7
April: [The Lord] has risen. [He is risen indeed.] Luke 24:6
May: Children, obey your parents. Ephesians 6:1
June: Jesus said, "I am the Good Shepherd." John 10:11
July: Jesus said, "Let the little children come to me." Mark 10:14
August: God created the heavens and the earth. Genesis 1:1

Year Two

September: Every word of God is [true]. Proverbs 30:5
October: Our Father who art in Heaven. Matthew 6:9
November: Give thanks to the Lord, for he is good. Psalm 136:1
December: [God] loves us and sent his Son. 1 John 4:10
January: Love one another. As I have loved you. John 13:34
February: A friend loves at all times. Proverbs 17:17
March: I am with you . . . wherever you go. Genesis 28:15
April: [Jesus] has risen, just as he said. Matthew 28:6
May: Children, obey your parents . . . This pleases the Lord. Colossians 3:20
June: [The Lord] gathers the lambs in his arms. . . . Isaiah 40:11
July: Jesus said, . . . "I am with you always." Matthew 28:20
August: The earth is the Lord's, and everything in it. Psalm 24:1

Year Three

September: Hear, O Israel: The Lord our God . . . is one. Deuteronomy 6:4
October: In the beginning God created the heavens and the earth. Genesis 1:1

November: The Lord is my Shepherd. I shall not be in want. Psalm 23:1

December: Today in the town of David a Savior has been born to you; he is Christ the Lord. Luke 2:11

January: And Jesus grew in wisdom and stature, and in favor with God and men. Luke 2:52

February: Be still, and know that I am God. Psalm 46:10

March: For God so loved the world that he gave his one and only Son. John 3:16

April: Jesus said . . . , "I am the resurrection and the life." John 11:25

May: [Jesus said,] "And surely I am with you always to the very end of the age." Matthew 28:20

June: Pray to the Lord our God. Jeremiah 37:3

July: Give thanks to the Lord, for he is good. Psalm 118:1

August: [God] hears our prayers. 1 Peter 3:12

Year Four

September: The heavens declare the glory of God. Psalm 19:1

October: And God spoke all these words: "I am the Lord your God." Exodus 20:1

November: Love the Lord your God with all your heart and with all your soul and with all your mind. Matthew 22:37

December: And [Mary] gave birth to her firstborn, a son. She wrapped him in cloths and placed him in a manger. Luke 2:7

January: After Jesus was born in Bethlehem, . . . Magi [came] to worship him. Matthew 2:1–2

February: [Jesus] got up, . . . and said to the waves, "Quiet! Be still!" then the wind died down and it was . . . calm. Mark 4:39

March: Jesus called the children to him and said, "Let the little children come to me." Luke 18:16

April: [The angel said,] "He is not here, he has risen!" Luke 24:6

May: Jesus said, "I am the good shepherd. I know my sheep and my sheep know me." John 10:14

June: [Noah] walked with God. Genesis 6:9

July: Pairs of . . . animals, . . . came to Noah and entered the ark. Genesis 7:8–9.

August: And God said, . . . "I have set my rainbow in the clouds, and it will be the sign of the covenant between me and the earth." Genesis 9:12–13

Year Five

September: . . . Give thanks to him and praise his name. For the Lord is good. Psalm 100:4b–5a.

October: . . . and surely I am with you always, to the very end of the age. Matthew 28:20b

November: Always give thanks to God the Father for everything, in the name of our Lord Jesus Christ. Ephesians 5:20

December: The people walking in darkness have seen a great light. Isaiah 9:2

January: The twelve disciples poem from *Jesus' 12 Disciples* by Louise Ulmer

February: Jesus answered, "I am the way, the truth, and the life. No one comes to the Father except through me." John 14:6

March: For God so loved the world that he gave his one and only Son, that whoever believes in him shall not perish but have eternal life. John 3:16

April and May: The Lord's Prayer

June: I will trust and not be afraid. Isaiah 12:2

July: Jesus said to them, "Go into all the world and preach the good news to all creation." Mark 16:15

August: Keep your tongues from evil and your lips from speaking lies. Psalm 34:13

Year Six

September: Praise the Lord . . . I will praise the Lord all my life. I will sing praise to my God as long as I live. Psalm 146:1a and 2

October: God called to [Moses] from within the bush, "Moses! Moses! Take off your sandals, for the place where you are standing is holy ground." Exodus 3:4–5

November: And God spoke all these words: "I am the Lord your God . . . You shall have no other gods before me." Exodus 20:1–3

December: Mary said: "My soul glorifies the Lord and my spirit rejoices in God my Savior." Luke 1:46–47

January: [Jesus] revealed his glory, and his disciples put their faith in him. John 2:11

February: Those who were in the boat worshiped him, saying, "Truly you are the Son of God." Matthew 14:32

March: Jesus said, "Everything is possible for him who believes." Mark 9:23

April: [The angel said, "Jesus] is not here; he has risen! Remember how he told you, while he was still with you in Galilee. Luke 24:6

May: Then Jesus told [Thomas], "Because you have seen me, you have believed; blessed are those who have not seen and yet have believed." John 20:29

June: The Lord is the everlasting God, the Creator of the ends of the earth. Isaiah 40:28

July: Cast all your cares on [Jesus] because he cares for you. 1 Peter 5:7

August: The grace of the Lord Jesus be with God's people. Amen. Revelation 22:21

54

Suggested Six-Year Curriculum

The following sources of stories are used in this six-year curriculum:

Leading Children in Worship (LCW) by Helene G. Zwyghuizen (Grand Rapids, Mich.: Baker Books, 1994)

Leading Children in Worship, Book 2 (LCW2) by Helene G. Zwyghuizen (Grand Rapids, Mich.: Baker Books, 1996)

Little Lambs by Sheri Triezenberg and Susan K. Verwys, 2 volumes of thirty stories each (Grand Rapids, Mich.: Church Development Resources, a Ministry of CRC Home Missions, 2850 Kalamazoo Avenue S.E., 1992)

Young Children and Worship (YC+W) by Sonja M. Stewart and Jerome W. Berryman (Louisville, Ky.: Westminster/ John Knox Press, 1989)

Age Groups

If you have enough children at each age and/or grade level, set up a Worship Center for each year. Use Year One with the two year olds, Year Two with the three year olds, Year Three with the four year olds, Year Four with the kindergartners, Year Five with the first graders, and Year Six with the second graders. You can adjust the whole curriculum up one year if you do not begin with the two year olds.

If you do not have enough children for each age to have its own Worship Center, you can combine two or more age or grade levels in one center. The two and three year olds, however, should each have their own Worship Center. We combine the four year olds and the kindergartners and for their curriculum, alternate Year Three and Year Four. We combine the first and second graders and for their curriculum, alternate Year Five and Year Six. If you combine more than two age or grade levels, tell each years' stories in rotation so the children eventually hear all of the stories.

The number of stories between Christmas and Lent will have to be adjusted each year since the date for Easter changes every year. If there are fewer Sundays in a particular year, take out the Bible stories the children have heard before. If there are more Sundays between Christmas and Lent, add the children's favorite Bible stories.

If you use the children-in-worship ministry in a year-round program, it is advisable to have substitute leaders available to allow the regular leaders time off several times during the year.

Years One and Two

Use the Bible stories and appropriate activities from *Little Lambs* and put them into the children-in-worship outline (see pages 23–27). Use the figure patterns in chapter 47 to make the wooden figures.

If you do not wish to use *Little Lambs,* or your children have had no previous exposure to the children-in-worship approach, then begin with these stories:

Lesson	Title	Source
1	Orientation Lesson 1	YC+W
2	Orientation Lesson 2	YC+W
3	Orientation Lesson 3	YC+W
4	Good Shepherd	YC+W
5	Good Shepherd/Lost Sheep	YC+W
6	Creation	YC+W
7	Creation cards	LCW2, chap. 55
8	The Garden of Eden, the Fall, and the Promise	LCW
9	Noah	YC+W
10	Abram and Sarai	YC+W
11	David, the Shepherd	LCW

After lesson 11, go to lesson 12 of year three. If you follow this plan, you will have a four-year curriculum.

Year Three

1	Orientation lesson 2	YC+W
2	Orientation lesson 3	YC+W
3	Creation	YC+W
4	Creation cards	LCW2, chap. 55
5	The Garden of Eden, the Fall, and the Promise	LCW
6	Noah	YC+W
7	Abram and Sarai	YC+W
8	David, the Shepherd	LCW
9	Elisha and the Room	LCW
10	Jonah	LCW2
11	Thanksgiving collage	LCW2, chap. 55
12	Advent 1/Prophecy (told without the candles)	YC+W
13	Advent 2/Annunciation	YC+W
14	Advent 3/Shepherds	YC+W
15	Advent 4/Wise Men	YC+W
16	Nativity/Birth of the Christ Child	YC+W
17	*My Book about Christmas*	See LCW2, chap. 56
18	The Boy Jesus in the Temple	YC+W
19	Jesus Is Baptized	YC+W
20	Jesus in the Wilderness	YC+W

Lesson	Title	Source
21	Feeding the Five Thousand	LCW
22	Calming the Storm	LCW
23	Jairus' Daughter	LCW
24	Review the previous six stories	
25	The Lent lessons begin here— Lenten puzzle	YC+W
26	Parables—Mustard Seed	YC+W
27	The Good Samaritan	YC+W
28	The Good Shepherd and the Wolf	YC+W
29	Jesus Is King	YC+W
30	Jesus' Last Passover	YC+W
31	Easter—The Garden Appearance	LCW
32	Easter—The Appearance on the Road to Emmaus	LCW
33	Easter—Jesus Appears to the Ten Disciples	LCW
34	Easter—Jesus Appears to the Disciples and Thomas	LCW
35	Easter—The Appearance at the Sea of Galilee	LCW
36	Easter—The Ascension	LCW
37	Pentecost	YC+W

Summer Lessons

38	We Talk with God in Prayer	LCW2
39, 40, 41	Three follow-up lessons	LCW2, chap. 55
42	We Talk with God at Home	LCW2
43	Follow-up lesson	LCW2, chap. 55
44	We Talk with God at Church	LCW2
45, 46	Follow-up lessons	LCW2, chap. 55
47	We Talk with God Everywhere	LCW2
48	Follow-up lesson	LCW2, chap. 55

Year Four

1	Orientation lesson 2	YC+W
2	Orientation lesson 3	YC+W

Lesson	Title	Source
3	Moses' Birth	LCW
4	Exodus	YC+W
5	Manna and Water	LCW2
6	Moses' Helpers	LCW2
7	The Ten Best Ways to Live	YC+W
8	Promised Land	YC+W
9	Review the six previous stories	
10	Thanksgiving collage	LCW2, chap. 55
11	Wise Men and Star	LCW2, chap. 55
12	Angels and Shepherds	LCW2, chap. 55
13	Inn and Stable	LCW2, chap. 55
14	Mary and Joseph	LCW2, chap. 55
15	Baby Jesus	LCW2, chap. 55
16	The Visit of the Wise Men	LCW
17	Anna and Simeon	LCW
18	Make "Jesus, the Boy" books	LCW2, chap. 55
19	Feeding the Five Thousand	LCW
20	Calming the Storm	LCW
21	Jairus' Daughter	LCW
22	The Good Shepherd and the Lost Sheep	YC+W
23	Make own Good Shepherd parable	LCW2, chap. 55
24	The Good Samaritan	YC+W
25	First lesson for Lent— Jesus' Temptations	YC+W
26	Jesus and the Children	YC+W
27	Jesus and Bartimaeus	YC+W
28	Jesus and Zacchaeus	YC+W
29	Jesus the King	YC+W
30	Jesus' Last Passover	YC+W
31	Easter booklets	LCW2, chap. 56
32	Real Easter eggs	LCW2, chap. 55
33	The Good Shepherd and the Wolf	YC+W
34	The Good Shepherd and the Lord's Supper 1	YC+W
35	The Good Shepherd and the Lord's Supper 2	YC+W
36	Ascension booklets	LCW2, chap. 56
37	Pentecost—use Lego World people	YC+W

Summer Lessons

Lesson	Title	Source
38	Noah Loves God	LCW2
39	Follow-up lesson	LCW2, chap. 55
40	Noah Obeys God	LCW2
41	Follow-up lesson	LCW2, chap. 55

Lesson	Title	Source
42	Two by Two	LCW2
43	Follow-up lesson	LCW2, chap. 55
44	Noah Is Safe	LCW2
45	Follow-up Lesson	LCW2, chap. 55
46	Noah Thanks God	LCW2
47	Follow-up lesson	LCW2, chap. 55
48	Noah	YC+W

Year Five

1	Review and Praise God	LCW
2	Abram and Sarai	YC+W
3	Make own figures and stones	LCW2, chap. 55
4	Birth of Isaac	LCW
5	God Destroys Sodom	LCW2
6	Isaac and Rebekah	LCW2
7	Esau and Jacob	LCW2
8	Jacob's Dream	LCW2
9	Review the previous six stories	
10	Thanksgiving booklets	LCW2, chap. 56
11	Advent 1/Prophets (told using the candles)	YC+W
12	Advent 2/Annunciation	YC+W
13	Advent 3/Shepherds	YC+W
14	Advent 4/Wise Men	YC+W
15	Nativity/The Birth of the Christ Child	YC+W
16	About Epiphany booklets	LCW2, chap. 56
17	Choosing Twelve Disciples	LCW
18	Make booklets of the previous story	LCW2, chap. 55
19	Jesus Heals a Paralytic	LCW2
20	Jesus Heals Ten Men	LCW2
21	The Good Shepherd and the Lost Sheep	YC+W
22	Lost Coin	LCW2
23	Lost Son	LCW2
24	Lent series—Lazarus	LCW2
25	Mary and Martha	LCW2
26	The Rich Man	LCW2
27	Zacchaeus	LCW2
28	Mary	LCW2
29	Jesus Prays	LCW2
30	Easter—Shining Star Big Book and Frieze	LCW2, chap. 56
31	Prayer Series— The Lord's Prayer	LCW2
32	The Persistent Widow	LCW2
33	Jesus' Example of Prayer	LCW2
34	The Pharisee and the Publican	LCW2
35	Ascension Sunday	LCW2, chap. 55
36	Pentecost	LCW2, chap. 55

Lesson	Title	Source
Summer Lessons		
37	Prayer booklets	LCW2, chap. 56
38	The Lame Man	LCW
39	Stephen	LCW2
40	Read the Arch Book: *Stephen, The First Martyr*	
41	Philip and the Ethiopian	LCW
42	Read the Arch Book: *Philip and the Ethiopian*	
43	Dorcas	LCW
44	Read the Arch Book: *Dorcas Sews for Others*	
45	Peter's Dream	LCW
46	Peter in Jail	LCW
47	Read the Arch Book: *Peter Set Free*	
48	Make booklets about the Acts stories or use the activity pages in *Peter* by Melissa C. Downey and Susan L. Lingo	LCW2, chap. 55, 56

Year Six

Lesson	Title	Source
1	Review and Praise God	LCW
2	Moses' Birth	LCW
3	Burning Bush	LCW2
4	The Ten Plagues	LCW2
5	Exodus	YC+W
6	The Ten Best Ways to Live	YC+W
7	The Ark and a Tent for God	YC+W
8	The Twelve Spies	LCW2
9	The Promised Land	YC+W
10	Review the previous eight stories	
11	Advent chains	LCW2, chap. 55, 56
12	Birth of John	LCW
13	Mary Visits Elizabeth	LCW2
14	Christmas	LCW2
15	Make Nativity scene	LCW2, chap. 55
16	Make Bible times homes	LCW2, chap. 55
17	Second week making homes	
18	Jesus' First Miracle	LCW2
19	Jesus Heals Peter's Mother-in-Law	LCW2

Lesson	Title	Source
20	Jairus' Daughter	LCW
21	Feeding the Five Thousand	LCW
22	Jesus Walks on Water	LCW2
23	Lazarus	LCW
24	Lent Series—Raising a Widow's Son	LCW2
25	Transfiguration	LCW2
26	Healing the Young Boy	LCW2
27	Cleansing the Temple	LCW2
28	Widow's Mite	LCW2
29	Washing the Disciples' Feet	LCW2
30	Easter—The Garden Appearance	LCW
31	The Appearance on the Road to Emmaus	LCW
32	Jesus Appears to the Ten Disciples	LCW
33	Jesus Appears to the Disciples and Thomas	LCW
34	The Appearance at the Sea of Galilee	LCW
35	Ascension	LCW
36	Pentecost (using people figures from other countries)	YC+W, LCW2, chap. 47
Summer Lessons		
37	Use the ideas for Pentecost in *Church Educator*, April 1993	LCW2, chap. 55
38	Saul Believes in Jesus	LCW
39	Read the Arch Book: *Paul Believes in Jesus*	
40	Paul and Barnabas	LCW
41	Paul's Helpers	LCW
42	Paul and Lydia	LCW
43	Paul and Silas in Jail	LCW2
44	Read the Arch Book: *The Jailer Who Changed His Mind*	
45	Paul's Shipwreck	LCW
46	Read the Arch Book: *Paul's Journeys*	
47	Activities from *Paul* by Melissa C. Downey and Susan L. Lingo	LCW2, chap. 55
48	Make booklets of the stories from Acts or have the children retell the stories to each other.	

55

Ideas and Activities

The ideas and activities in this chapter follow the order of the curriculum in chapter 54. The children take their projects home where they can use them to retell the story.

Year Three

Creation Ideas

Spend two weeks on the creation story. The second week make creation cards using 4″ x 6″ file cards.

Use any of the following ideas:

1. Have all the pieces cut out for the children so all they have to do is paste the pieces on the cards. Their finished project will look like the cards you use.
2. Have available the following:

> Day 1—Yellow paper cut to 1/2 the size of the card and dark blue paper cut to 1/2 the size of the card. The children glue the paper on the card.
> Day 2—White arch shape for the children to glue on the card. The children can color their cards blue first.
> Day 3—Brown shape for the earth; the children add the rest.
> Day 4—Have 1/2 dark blue piece of paper, self-stick stars, and a yellow sun. The children can draw the moon.
> Day 5—Children can draw fish and birds.
> Day 6—Children can draw animals and people.

3. Let the children draw and/or color everything themselves.

Be sure the backs of the cards are numbered so the children can put them in the correct order.

Thanksgiving Ideas

Make individual or group collages of things the children are thankful for by cutting out pictures from magazines, sale papers, or catalogs and pasting them to poster board, large manilla sheets, or newsprint. (Ask your local newspaper printer for the ends of their newsprint rolls.) Hang finished collages in the church foyer for everyone to enjoy.

"We Talk with God in Prayer"

Activity on the Sunday the Bible story is told:

Have the children begin cutting out pictures of things they are thankful for. Or the children could color pictures of things to be thankful for and cut those out.

The children should keep their pictures in their cubbyholes to use when they put "My Thank-You Book" together.

Three Follow-up Lessons

1. Have several pages of colored construction paper stapled together. Title each booklet "My Thank-You Book." Have the children glue into their books the pictures they cut out when they had the "We Talk with God in Prayer" lesson.

   Label each picture. The children could "read" their books to each other.

2. Let the children make place mats by pasting construction-paper fruit/food onto plain, white paper place mats. Or find fruit/food stickers and let the children use those to decorate their place mats. Make enough so that each person in the child's family will have a place mat.

   While making the place mats, talk about how we are thankful to God for all this food.

   Patterns for food can be found in the *Preschool Pattern Book* by Linda Blassingame, Romelda Dilley, Pat Karch, and Olga Packard; and the *Elementary Pattern Book* by Dan Grossmann.

3. Do this activity after the lesson "We Talk with God in Prayer" on the first Sunday with nice weather. Take the children outside for a walk. Let them look for things to be thankful for.

   Provide paper bags that the children can use for collecting stones, twigs, blades of grass, dandelions, etc. After returning to the Worship Center, talk about the things collected and say "Thank you God for _____." (Provide newspapers for the children to put their things on so the room will not get messy!)

"We Talk with God at Home"

Activity on the Sunday the Bible story is told:

Have each child make a clock. For each child provide:

> a paper plate numbered to resemble a clock face
> 2 clock hands
> a paper-fastener
> a copy of the following poem
> > Anytime, anywhere
> > I can talk to God.
> > When I'm glad,

When I'm sad
I can talk to God.

Help the children paste the poem on the face of the clock. Add the hands to the clock and remind the children that they can pray to God just like Aaron, Miriam, and Moses did and that the clock will remind them to pray.

They may wish to add further decorations to their clocks.

Follow-up Lesson

Have each child make a booklet about his or her family:

Title page: We Talk with God
page 1: a picture of a home
page 2: a picture of a family praying at mealtime
page 3: a picture of a person praying at bedtime
page 4: a picture of a daddy
page 5: a picture of a mommy
page 6: a picture of a boy or a girl
page 7 and beyond: add as many pages as there are children in the child's family—one page per family member.

Punch the pages and tie with yarn.

People I See in God's World by Cindy Maddox is a book depicting parents doing different kinds of jobs. If you know the occupations of each child's parents you can photocopy the appropriate pictures to make each child's booklet unique to him or her. This book also has pictures of children.

"We Talk with God at Church"

Activity on the Sunday the Bible story is told:

Color or draw pictures of churches. Talk about going to church and what everyone does at church.

Follow-up Lessons

1. Take a walk to the sanctuary and talk about the furniture, the decorations, and what everyone does in the sanctuary.
2. Make a prayer mobile. For each child provide:

   pictures of a child, Bible, church, praying hands, church window
   a wire clothes hanger
   yarn
   scissors
   crayons or markers

   Have the children color the pictures with crayons or markers and then cut out the pictures. (Before cutting, you may want to glue the pictures to poster board or construction paper so the pieces are heavier.) Punch a hole in the top of each picture. Attach a piece of yarn to each picture and tie the yarn to the clothes hanger.

Use *Bible and Everyday Pictures to Color* by Marian Bennett to photocopy pictures of a Bible, church, children, and families.

"We Talk with God Everywhere"

Activities on the Sunday the Bible story is told:

1. Color pictures about Paul's journey.
2. Make boats. For each child provide:

> Eight-ounce round margarine container
> 10" drinking straw
> small sail made of paper
> Play Doh or modeling clay

Let the children color the sail. Tape along the top end of the straw. Push the straw into a piece of Play Doh or clay placed in the bottom of the container.

Follow-up Lesson

Have a large piece of colored construction paper for each child. Fold it in half to represent a suitcase. Let the children cut out pictures of clothes, shoes, towels, and other things they would put in a suitcase. Have them paste the pictures in their suitcase or staple the sides of the construction paper and have the children put the pictures they cut out into the suitcase.

Talk about God's going with us when we take a vacation and being with us wherever we are.

Repeat the Bible verse: "God hears our prayer" (1 Pet. 3:12). Write the verse on the outside of each child's suitcase.

Year Four

Thanksgiving Ideas

Use the ideas from Year Three. If you make a class collage one year, make individual collages the following year.

Advent and Nativity Ideas

The Christmas Story is a big book and frieze published by Shining Star Publication. Use the ideas you find appropriate to your Worship Center that are included in the lesson plan book. Since there are six lessons and only four Sundays in Advent, we combine lesson one, "The Wise Men," and lesson three, "The

Star," on the first Sunday and conclude on the first Sunday of Christmas with the "Baby Jesus" lesson.

"Jesus, the Boy" booklets: Warner Press publishes reproducible coloring books with pages about Christmas, the Wise Men's visit, and Jesus' visit to the temple at age twelve. Make a booklet for each child, talk about what happened to Jesus, have the children color their pages and/or send them home to be colored.

The children could also draw their own pictures about Jesus and put them together as a booklet.

Good Shepherd Parable Story Ideas

1. Use 1/2 sheet green poster board per child. Let the children cut out blue water and dark shapes from construction paper. Cut one sheet brown construction paper per child into one-inch widths for the sheep fold. (Using a paper cutter ahead of time is easier.) Copy one sheet per child of the shepherd and sheep figures so they can retell the story to each other and at home. Cover the shepherd and sheep ahead of time with clear Con-Tact paper.
2. Spray paint the outside of a manilla folder gold (one per child). Paste green construction paper on the inside (or spray paint it green). Let the children cut out the blue water and rock shapes from construction paper. Cut one sheet brown construction paper per child into one-inch widths for the sheep fold. (Using a paper cutter ahead of time is easier.) Copy one sheet per child of the shepherd and sheep. Cover with clear Con-Tact paper. The water, rocks, fold, and figures can be kept in an envelope inside the folder when not being used. This is easier to carry and store than using the poster board. (This idea comes from Trudy Williams.)
3. Provide a cover with the Good Shepherd picture on it, one sheet of blue paper, one of green paper, and as many other sheets as you deem appropriate for each child. Provide sheep stickers. Have a large sheep on the last page for the children to write their own name on. Let the children make their own booklets about the Good Shepherd story. Staple the pages together.
4. Spray paint a small shoe box gold (one per child). Let the children cut their own water, rock, and sheep fold pieces from felt. Provide the shepherd and sheep figures slightly reduced in size for each child. (We used this with older children so they would have their own story materials. It was just the right size for them to tell the story on their beds before going to sleep at night.)

Real Easter Eggs*

Fill eight large plastic Easter eggs with the following:

Egg #1
Contents: Palm branch
Scripture: Matthew 21:8–9

*Basic idea adapted from page 57 of *Before and After Easter* by Debbie Trafton O'Neal.

Egg #2
Contents: Plate
Scripture: Matthew 26:26–28

Egg #3
Contents: Cross
Scripture: Matthew 27:31–35

Egg #4
Contents: White cloth
Scripture: Matthew 27:57–59

Egg #5
Contents: Stone
Scripture: Matthew 27:60

Egg #6
Contents: Spices
Scripture: Mark 16:1

Egg #7
Contents: Angel
Scripture: Matthew 28:1–3, 5–7

Egg #8
Contents: Empty
Scripture: Luke 24:1–9

Number each egg on the outside. Place eggs in a large basket. Let each child choose one and open it in turn. Talk about how the contents help us understand what happened to Jesus and what he did for us. Read the Scripture passage after each egg is opened.

Pentecost

The Lego Company has a set of world people that works well with the Pentecost story.

"Noah Loves God"

Activity on the Sunday the Bible story is told:

Make the "Helping Others" scroll. Using a 12″-wide, 6′-long piece of newsprint, write down the ideas the children have on what we can do to help others. When finished, tape the ends of the paper to empty paper towel rolls, roll up from each end like a scroll and tie with yarn. Review these ideas over the summer and remind the children to keep helping others.

Follow-up Lesson

Read "Noah's Big Boat" from *Read-Aloud Bible Stories,* vol. 3. Begin coloring one of the books or one of the other extra activities connected with the Noah stories.

"Noah Obeys God"

Activity on the Sunday the Bible story is told:

Show the measurements of the ark on the church parking lot or on the school playground or other large area. It was 450 feet long, 75 feet wide, and three stories or 45 feet high.

Follow-up Lesson

Make arks from shoe boxes. Paint boxes brown or tan. Use crayons or markers to draw wooden boards on the sides. Cut door in one side. Carefully fold down. Use lids as the roof. Leaving a 1″ width around the edge of shoe box cover, cut out the middle. Use poster board the length of the hole and twice its width. Fold in the middle. Tape to the cover on the inside to make a roof. Use markers or crayons to draw boards on the roof.

"Two by Two"

Activity on the Sunday the Bible story is told:

Make animals to put in the arks. Patterns can be found in the *Preschool Pattern Book* by Linda Blassingame, Romelda Dilley, Pat Karch, and Olga Packard and the *Elementary Pattern Book* by Dan Grossmann. Copy the animal patterns you want. Hold these animal patterns up to a window and trace them on the back of the sheet of paper. Retrace the animals on another sheet of paper. Have the children color and cut out the animals. The pair of animals will stand up if you staple them to a toilet-tissue roll, cut in half. The pair of animals should be going in the same direction.

Follow-up Lesson
1. Continue making animals for the arks.
2. For the feast: spread graham crackers with frosting. Set animal cookies, two by two, into the frosting.

"Noah Is Safe"

Activity on the Sunday the Bible story is told:

Fill a number of clear plastic jars half-full of water. Add blue food coloring. Round corners of small Ivory soap bars. Put soap in jars and screw on lids. Children can shake the jars to create a "storm" and the "ark" will always float.

Follow-up Lesson

Read *The Big Book of Noah's Ark* by Stacie Strong.

"Noah Thanks God"

Three ways to make a rainbow:

1. Fold a paper towel twice, creating a square. Dip each corner into red, blue, yellow, and green food coloring. This results in an interesting design when the dried towel is unfolded.
2. Have the children dip cotton balls into dry powdered tempera. Then brush the cotton balls on wet paper. A spring-type clothespin may be attached to the cotton ball for ease in holding.
3. Let the children shake dry powdered tempera from a salt shaker onto wet paper.

Make a copy of a rainbow with a cloud at the bottom for each child. (Reproduce on heavy paper, if possible.) Let children trace or print their names on the clouds. Punch a hole near the top and hang from the ceiling.

Additional Activities and Ideas

1. Puzzles—"Lauri" puzzles or "Shining Star" puzzles of the Noah story
2. Noah's Ark Dominos
3. Flannel board—Use the Noah's story figures backed with flannel
4. Noah's Memory Match-up Game
5. Noah's ark wallpaper border to decorate the room
6. The ark and the animals storybooks—let the children make pictures and/or books using stickers
7. Color large erasable pictures on the floor
8. Have several different arks and animal sets and let the children retell the story to each other

Year Five

Abram and Sarai

For the second week on the Abram and Sarai story, make stand-up figures of Abraham and Sarah (trace the wooden figures on poster board, cut out, and glue stands to the back). Give children copies of an Old Testament map with Ur, Haran, Shechem, Bethel, Hebron circled. Children can make stones for altars out of Play Doh or homemade dough.

We tell the Abram and Sarai story on a simple map underlay that includes the cities of Ur, Haran, Bethel, Shechem, Hebron, the country of Egypt, the Tigris and Euphrates Rivers, and the Mediterranean Sea. Abram would have followed the fertile crescent so he had water for his flocks and herds. We begin the story in Ur because of the following Bible references to God calling Abram: Genesis 11:28–31; 15:7 and following; Nehemiah 9:7; and Acts 7:1–4 (Stephen's speech). If you choose to do this, adjust the story to include Ur.

How to make a map underlay: On a clear overhead sheet trace the map you wish to use. Project the map onto a cream-colored underlay. Trace the outline of the map on the underlay with permanent markers in appropriate colors.

Choosing Twelve Disciples Booklet Ideas

1. Retell the story, stopping to let the children draw each disciple. Put pages together for individual booklets.
2. Let children each choose one or two disciples to draw (depending on class size) and make a class booklet.
3. Use what you feel is appropriate for your children from pages 18–31 of *Jesus Prepares to Serve* by Tracy Leffingwell Harrast.

Easter

Easter is similar to the *Christmas* big book and frieze published by Shining Star. Use what you feel is appropriate.

Prayer Series

Do these activities to remind the children to pray. All should be taken home to use. Do one activity per week with each story and allow the children who miss an activity to do it on the catch-up week.

1. "Table Blessing," found on pages 52–53 of *52 Ways to Teach Children to Pray*. The outlines are drawn on poster board and the cut made in the saucer. The children cut the cup and saucer out, paste the prayer on, and decorate them. (Tip: Tape the cup tabs underneath the saucer to help it stand up better.) This is a reminder for the children to pray at mealtime.
2. "Prayer Alphabet" from page 45 of *52 Ways to Teach Children to Pray*. Write the alphabet down one side of an 8-1/2″ x 14″ sheet of paper, one sheet for each child. The children fill it in with things to either pray about or be thankful for beginning with each letter. An adult helps with spelling.
3. "Prayer Booklets"—prayers to use at various times are copied; one set per child. Each child assembles a booklet, ties it with yarn, and reads through the prayers with an adult helper. A more elaborate idea is found on page 30 of *52 Ways to Teach Children to Pray*.
4. A wall hanging, found on page 91 of *Celebrate Jesus*. Use white felt for the banner, with a small hem sewn on the top for a dowel. The suns (orange felt), mountains (green felt), and letters (various colors of felt) are cut out ahead of time. Each child chooses the color they want, glues the pieces down, slips the dowel in, and makes a hanger from cord or twine. The children may hang these in their rooms as reminders to pray morning and evening.

Ascension Day

Retell the prayer stories to children who missed them and/or do the prayer activity they missed. Read the Ascension story from Acts during the closing circle time.

Pentecost

Use *Jesus Prays and Teaches Us to Pray* from the American Bible Society. Read as many sections as time allows. Read the Pentecost story from Acts during the closing circle time.

Summer Sessions for Years Five and Six

To lighten up the summers, tell fewer stories and use books and other activities related to the stories.

The Standard Publishing Company has published two books, *Peter* and *Paul* that can be used nicely during the summer. Children can draw their own pictures to go with the stories, file them, and at the end of the summer put them together in booklets. Warner Press has reproducible coloring pages to go with the Acts stories.

Year Six

Advent Chains

Several are available from Creative Communications for the Parish:

"Chase a Star"—examines biblical depictions of stars
"Joy to the World"—about traditions and customs in other countries but based on Luke 2
"The Savior Is Coming"—each link explains a biblical name of Jesus
"Let's Go to Bethlehem"—beginning with Adam and Eve, biblical names are added until, on December 23, "you" is added, and December 24 "Jesus" is added.

Make the chains during worship time and send them home, encouraging the children to remove one link each day until Christmas.

Make Nativity Scene

Use old Christmas cards. The children cut out Mary, Joseph, shepherds, sheep, other animals, a manger, and an angel. Cut a 1/2″-wide strip for each figure from the unused part of the card. Bend into a circle. Either staple or tape to bottom of each figure. Tape or staple two rings to the bottom at each side of a manger scene to use as a backdrop.

The children can tell the Christmas story to each other and then take their figures and scene home to retell the story to their family members. The children can keep these and make them part of their yearly family Christmas decorations.

Bible Times Homes

Use pages 18, 22–24 from *Jesus Grows Up* by Tracey Leffingwell Harrast to make the home. Use pages 38 and 39 for the closing time. Instead of covering the shoe box and pudding box with paper, spray paint them tan ahead of time. You do not need to coat the bottoms with glue and soil.

Miracles of Jesus

If you use the Lazarus story here, use a green underlay and leave out the words about Lent at the beginning of the story and the wondering time thoughts about Lent at the end.

Lent Idea

Make a cross on a 8-1/2″ x 14″ sheet of purple paper. Have the children cut out the cross. Mount on heavy white paper. Each week provide a small picture of the story for the day. You may want to take the pictures from your Bible markers, reduce them slightly, and draw a circle around each. The children can cut out one picture each week. Paste these on the cross; week one at the top, week two on the left cross arm, week three on the right cross arm, weeks four, five, and six down the bottom piece of the cross. On the last Sunday talk about how each of these stories helps us to get ready for Easter. Give each child a butterfly to put on the middle of the cross and talk about how the butterfly is a symbol of Easter. Encourage the children to take their crosses home and tell the stories to their parents.

Pentecost: Good News!*

Good news! When Jesus ascended to heaven forty days after the resurrection, he promised to send the Holy Spirit to empower his followers to become his witnesses in Jerusalem, in all Judea and Samaria, and to the ends of the earth (Acts 1:8). This miracle, the descent of the Holy Spirit, took place on the Jewish Pentecost, observed fifty days after Passover, and a group of frightened disciples hiding in Jerusalem were empowered to become fearless witnesses, even in the face of opposition by the civil authorities. Share the good news that those who follow Jesus today, too, have been empowered by the Holy Spirit and have been given the ability to carry on Jesus' mission and ministry in their particular situations and circumstances.

Since news today is often acquired by reading the newspaper, all learning activities in this article involve the use of this medium. Just as any good reporter would learn more about the story by asking "Who, What, When, Where, Why, and How," the children will also discover information about Pentecost and its

*"Pentecost: Good News!" by Judith Harris Chase and Phyllis Vos Wezeman is from *Church Educators,* April 1993. Used with permission.

significance in their lives by participating in six activities, involving eight projects, centering on these questions.

When: Newspaper Beads

Supplies: newspaper, scissors, glue, red yarn or ribbon, ruler, pencils

Fifty days after the resurrection of their friend, the followers of Jesus were gathered in an upstairs room in Jerusalem where they had been staying. Pentecost, from the Greek word *pentekoste* meaning fiftieth, was observed by the Jewish people fifty days after Passover. Called *Shavout,* meaning weeks in Hebrew, the holiday is observed seven weeks, or fifty days, after Passover. Often called Harvest Festival, Festival of the First Fruits, and Festival of the Giving of the Torah, it was originally an agricultural festival. *Shavout* was one of three occasions when people were required to go to the Temple in Jerusalem with offerings from their farms. After the destruction of the second Temple in the first century, the people could no longer bring their offerings to the Temple so the festival was designated as the anniversary of the reception of the Torah at Mt. Sinai. At synagogue services, the Ten Commandments are recited and the book of Ruth is read.

Since the number fifty is significant to both the Jewish and the Christian meaning of the day, commemorate Pentecost by making fifty beads of newspaper strips. Each class member can form several beads to add to this collection, or the project may be started in the learning center and continued at home so that each person has a necklace. Use colored comic pages or newspaper sections with colored paper or print. Cut long triangles eight inches long with a one-inch base. The triangle strips should taper to a point. Wrap the triangle's base around a pencil, brush on glue and continue rolling the paper to the end. Slide the pencil out and allow the paper to dry. Repeat until fifty beads are finished. String onto red yarn or ribbon and add to a Pentecost worship table or bulletin board display or wear the beads and share the "Good News" with people who remark about them.

What: Windsock, Candle, and Language Collage

While Jesus' followers were gathered together on the day of Pentecost, there suddenly came a sound like the rush of a strong wind, which filled the house. Tongues, as of fire, appeared, and one rested on each of the people. All were filled with the Holy Spirit and began to speak in other languages, as the Spirit gave them the ability.

Explore these three themes and symbols—wind, flame, and language—by using the following activities.

Wind—*supplies:* newspaper, red construction paper, scissors, stapler, ruler, yarn or string, paper punch

Create a windsock to represent the wind that came upon those assembled. Fold one entire sheet of newspaper at its crease. Fringe the paper by cutting one inch slits starting at the open edge and ending two inches before the fold. Cut a band of red construction paper 18 inches by 1 inch. Staple red paper to the folded edge of the newspaper fringe. Fold back any paper that extends beyond the end of the red strip. Punch holes on each side of the red band. Tie yarn or string to the holes. Then hang the windsock where breezes will allow it to move.

Flames—*supplies:* newspaper, red or orange tissue paper, tape, glue

Flames on candles can be reminders of the symbol of flames mentioned in the Pentecost story, Acts 2. Fold a double sheet of newspaper in half. Form a candle shape by rolling a cylinder of newspaper. Tape at the top and bottom so the candle will hold its shape, or tuck the newspaper into itself. Glue a red or orange tissue paper puff to the top to represent the flame. Finished candles can become part of a display featuring Pentecost symbols.

Languages—*supplies:* newspapers and magazines in various languages, paper, scissors, glue

As a reminder of the many languages that were spoken on the day of Pentecost, explore a variety of newspapers and magazines from countries around the world. These are available from newsstands, book stores, and libraries. Assemble a collage by cutting words and articles from the papers and gluing them to a background piece. Add the completed project to a display of Pentecost symbols.

Who: Paper People

Supplies: newspaper, tape, scissors, crayons or markers

According to Acts 1:15, about 120 people were gathered together when the initial events of Pentecost occurred. Once they were filled with the Holy Spirit, this small group of empowered people went out to witness, or share the Good News with others. It is recorded in Acts 2:41 that after Peter's sermon about three thousand people welcomed his message and were baptized.

Cut a string of paper figures to represent the three thousand who joined the group of believers on Pentecost. Cut a strip as long as a double sheet of newspaper, and about 8 to 10 inches wide. Make 3-inch folds, pleating back and forth until the strip is used up. If a longer strip is needed, tape another sheet to the first and continue folding pleats. Draw a simple figure on the top panel. Be certain that parts of the figure extend over the folds on both sides (i.e., hands, bottom edges of clothing). Snip along the drawn lines, taking care to leave some of the folded areas intact. Carefully unfold the pleated shapes to reveal a string of paper people. Use markers or crayons to individualize the "new believers."

Why: Dove

Supplies: newspaper, glue, stapler, bulletin board covered with red paper or cloth

Because the followers of Jesus were filled with the Holy Spirit, they were empowered to tell others the Good News of the Gospel. Peter addressed the crowd and told them about the life, death, and resurrection of the Savior. Three thousand of the listeners responded to his message by believing and becoming baptized.

The dove is a familiar Pentecost symbol for the Holy Spirit. Cut or tear a large dove shape and fasten it to a bulletin board covered with red paper or cloth. Each class member can tear strips or ovals from newspaper for feathers. Fasten the feathers to the background dove by gluing or stapling. For a feathery look, attach torn strips so a portion is loose, fluttering out from the background.

How: Party Hats

Supplies: newspaper, trims, feathers, ribbons

How did the followers of Jesus respond to the events of Pentecost? Once they were filled with the Holy Spirit, they went and told others the Good News. Many people believed and were baptized, and the large group continued to meet together to praise God and to witness to more people. Pentecost is often called the birthday of the church.

Celebrate the birthday of the church by folding a party hat from newspaper. Fold a double sheet in half. Fold down the two top corners so they meet in the middle. On the top side turn up approximately two inches of the lower edge and then turn up again to form a cuff. Flip the hat over to form a cuff on the other side. Crease all folds so the hat will keep its shape. Add colorful paper trims, ribbon, or feathers to create a party hat. Wear the hat as part of a Pentecost celebration.

Where: Bookmarks

Supplies: newspaper, wide red ribbon or construction paper, scissors, cotton balls or tissue, tape, glue or stapler

Although the season of Easter ends when Pentecost begins, this special day provides the opportunity for people to consider where they will share the Good News of the Resurrection, and to consider what participation in Jesus' ministry means to them. Explore Scripture passages and learn more about Jesus' challenge to all believers. Also read the stories of people of faith who were empowered to participate in Jesus' ministry despite great personal cost. Some of these people include Dorothy Day, Martin Luther King Jr., and Mother Teresa.

Make a bookmark and use it to mark your place in the Pentecost story and as a tool to use when sharing the Good News with others. Use wide red ribbon or red construction paper strips. Cut two small newspaper hearts. Place a cotton ball or small wad of tissue between the heart pieces and glue or staple around the edges. Attach the heart to the top of the red strip. Make one to keep and several to share.

56

Resources

Books to Read

Animals: Two by Two. Batavia, Ill.: Lion Publishing, 1980.

The Ark and the Animals. Chicago: Moody Press, 1987.

Gambill, Henrietta D. *The First Zoo*. Cincinnati: The Standard Publishing Company, 1989.

Granger, Carol. *The Jailer Who Changed His Mind*. An Arch Book. St. Louis: Concordia Publishing House, 1971.

Hodges, Connie. *Stephen, The First Martyr*. An Arch Book. St. Louis: Concordia Publishing House, 1985.

Jander, Martha Streufert. *Philip and the Ethiopian*. An Arch Book. St. Louis: Concordia Publishing House, 1990.

Kolbrek, Loyal. *Paul Believes in Jesus*. An Arch Book. St. Louis: Concordia Publishing House, 1972.

————. *Paul's Journeys*. An Arch Book. St. Louis: Concordia Publishing House, 1988.

Latourette, Jean. *The Story of Noah's Ark*. An Arch Book. St. Louis: Concordia Publishing House, 1965.

L'Engle, Madeleine. *Anytime Prayers*. Wheaton, Ill.: Harold Shaw Publishers, 1994.

Lindvall, Ella K. *Read-Aloud Bible Stories*. Chicago: Moody Press, vol. 1, 1982; vol. 2, 1985; vol. 3, 1990; vol. 4, 1995.

Mara, Pam. *The Ark*. Anderson, Ind.: Warner Press, 1986.

Miller, Alberta Poth. *Dorcas Sews for Others*. An Arch Book. St. Louis: Concordia Publishing House, 1984.

Noah's Ark. Cincinnati: The Standard Publishing Company, 1991.

Spier, Peter. *Noah's Ark*. New York: Dell Publishing, 1992.

Stowell, Gordon, and Charlotte Stowell. *The Ark and Animals*. Chicago: Moody Press, 1987.

Strong, Stacie. *The Big Book of Noah's Ark*. Cincinnati: The Standard Publishing Company, 1990.

Truitt, Gloria. *Peter Set Free*. An Arch Book. St. Louis: Concordia Publishing House, 1991.

Ulmer, Louise. *Jesus' 12 Disciples*. An Arch Book. St. Louis: Concordia Publishing House, 1982.

Willis, Doris. *I Like to Come to My Church*. Bible Board Book. Nashville: Abingdon Press, 1990.

————. *We Give Thanks!* Bible Board Book. Nashville: Abingdon Press, 1991.

Books for Ideas

Daniel, Becky. *The Christmas Story*. Christian activity lessons with reproducible pages for ages 3–8. Carthage, Ill.: Shining Star Publications, 1990.

————. *Easter Week*. Christian activity lessons with reproducible pages for ages 3–8. Carthage, Ill.: Shining Star Publications, 1991.

————. *Moses and the Ten Commandments*. Christian activity lessons with reproducible pages for ages 3–8. Carthage, Ill.: Shining Star Publications, 1992.

————. *Noah's Story*. Christian activity lessons with reproducible pages for ages 3–8. Carthage, Ill.: Shining Star Publications, 1991.

Darling, Kathy. *Preschool Bible Crafts*. Carthage, Ill.: Shining Star Publications, 1992.

Downey, Melissa. *Paul*. Cincinnati: The Standard Publishing Company, 1993.

————. *Peter*. Cincinnati: The Standard Publishing Company, 1993.

Halverson, Delia. *Teaching Prayer in the Classroom*. Nashville: A Griggs Educational Resource. Abingdon Press, 1989.

Harrast, Tracy Leffingwell. *Jesus Grows Up*. Elgin, Ill.: David C. Cook Publishing Company, 1991.

————. *Jesus Prepares to Serve*. Elgin, Ill.: David C. Cook Publishing Company, 1991.

————. *Jesus Teaches Me to Pray*. Elgin, Ill.: David C. Cook Publishing Company, 1991.

Leone, Dee. *The Miracles of Jesus*. Carthage, Ill.: Shining Star Publications, 1990.

————. *The Stories of Noah and Joseph*. A Christian activity book with reproducible pages for ages 3–6. Carthage, Ill.: Shining Star Publications, 1988.

MacKenthum, Carole. *Poems, Prayers and Projects*. Carthage, Ill.: Shining Star Publications, 1984.

O'Neal, Debbie Trafton. *Before and After Easter*. Minneapolis: Augsburg Publishing House, 1992.

Senterfill, Marilyn. *Celebrate Jesus*. Carthage, Ill.: Shining Star Publications, 1988.

Williamson, Nancy S. *52 Ways to Teach Children to Pray*. San Diego: Rainbow Books, 1991.

Other Sources of Ideas and Materials

Coloring Books

Bennett, Marian. *Bible and Everyday Pictures to Color*. Cincinnati: The Standard Publishing Company, 1992.

Going to Church. Anderson, Ind.: Warner Press, 1975. Preschool dot-to-dot coloring book.

Maddox, Cindy. *People I See in God's World*. Anderson, Ind.: Warner Press, Inc., 1990.

Noah's Ark Two-of-a-Kind Activity Book. Anderson, Ind.: Warner Press, Inc.

Reproducible Bible Story Coloring Book. Old Testament and New Testament. Cincinnati: The Standard Publishing Company, 1994.

Smith, Dorothy. *The Story of Noah's Ark*. Anderson, Ind.: Warner Press, Inc., 1985.

Pattern Books

Blassingame, Linda, Romelda Dilley, Pat Karch, and Olga Packard, illustrators. *Preschool Pattern Book*. Cincinnati: The Standard Publishing Company, 1990.

Grossman, Dan, illustrator. *Elementary Pattern Book*. Cincinnati: The Standard Publishing Company, 1990.

Ark Pattern

Better Homes and Gardens Woodcrafts patterns. "All-Aboard Noah's Ark," designed by Bill and Jan Shirley. Order from Patterns, P.O. Box 8499, Clinton, IA 52736.

Puzzles

Noah Stories
    LR-2154   Rainbow
    LR-2175   Noah's Ark
Creation Story
    LR-2173   Dolphins
    LR-2152   Bird
    LR-2172   Cat 'n Kittens
    LR-2008   Stars and Moon
    LR-2122   School of Fish
Easter
    LR-2148   Easter Egg
    LR-2126   Butterflies
All available from Lauri, P.O. Box F, Phillips-Avon, ME 04966.

Write for a sample, catalog, and order blank from Shining Star Puzzles, Shining Star Publications, a division of Good Apple, Inc., Box 299, Carthage, IL 62321-0299.

Other Resources

American Bible Society produces booklets of Scripture passages to use with older children. Use "Jesus Prays and Teaches Us to Pray" in the prayer series with older children. American Bible Society, P.O. Box 5656, Grand Central Station, New York, NY 10164-0851.

The Channing L. Bete Co., Inc., 200 State Road, South Deerfield, MA 01272-0200, produces useful 8-1/2" x 11" scriptographic booklets for children. The following booklets are listed in the curriculum: year 3, lesson 17—"My Book about Christmas"; year 4, lesson 31—"Easter," lesson 36—"Jesus Goes to Heaven"; year 5, lesson 10—"Thanksgiving," lesson 16—"About Eiphany," lesson 37—"About Prayer." (Their two booklets "About Faith and Your Child," for ages birth to six years, and one for ages six to twelve years are excellent resources for parents.) Write for a sample, catalog, and order blank.

Creative Communications for the Parish, 10300 Watson Road, St. Louis, MO 63127, produces advent chain booklets and other resources. Write for a sample, catalog, and order blank.

Richards, Lawrence. *International Children's Bible Handbook.* Dallas: Word Publishing Company, 1989.

Words of Hope, a media ministry of the Reformed Church in America, Box 1706, Grand Rapids, MI 49501-1706, produces a video and worksheets about the modern-day spread of the gospel that can be used with the Bible stories from the Book of Acts used during the summers in Years Five and Six.

Help with Signing

Costello, Elaine. *Religious Signing.* New York: Bantam Books, 1986.
Riekhof, Lottie L. *The Joy of Signing.* Springfield, Mo.: Gospel Publishing House, 1987.